Contents

National
...tion Policy
...ng People

Office of the Minister for Children

September 2007

Copyright © Minister for Health and Children, 2007

Office of the Minister for Children
Department of Health and Children
Hawkins House
Hawkins Street
Dublin 2
Tel: +353 (0)1 635 4000
Fax: +353 (0)1 674 3223
E-mail: omc@health.gov.ie
Web: www.omc.gov.ie

Published by The Stationery Office, Dublin

ISBN: 0-7557-7557-0

Foreword

It is a great pleasure for me to launch the National Recreation Policy for Young People, aged between 12 and 18 years. The National Children's Strategy, *Our Children — Their Lives,* published in 2000, identified the need for more opportunities for community-based play, leisure and cultural activities. This was high on the list of issues raised by children themselves in the consultation process for the strategy.

The first part of the Government's response to this need was the creation of the National Play Policy, *Ready, Steady, Play!,* published in March 2004. Aimed primarily at children under the age of 12, its purpose was to create better play opportunities for young children. It also greatly improved our understanding of the importance and relevance of play for children. The work done by local authorities on the development of playgrounds, together with the promotion of play by the National Play Resource Centre, have both had a visible impact on the opportunities for play for younger children.

The National Recreation Policy represents the second stage in the fulfillment of the call, identified in the National Children's Strategy, for more play and recreational opportunities for young people. Called *Teenspace*, this policy is aimed at young people between the ages of 12 and 18, and provides a strategic framework for the promotion of better recreational opportunities for that age group. Extensive consultation has shown that the lack of recreational opportunities continues to be a major concern for young people throughout the country, while the research undertaken for the development of the policy has helped us to understand a lot more about what constitutes 'recreation' for young people today. This ranges from simply 'hanging out' with friends, to more casual activities, such as skateboarding or surfing the Net, to more formal structured activities, such as organised sports or music groups. The policy highlights the requirement for multi-agency support and input in order to meet the kinds of needs described by young people.

The National Recreation Policy has been developed with input from various Government departments and agencies, all of which will have a crucial role to play in the delivery of the policy. It joins up and identifies the ways in which to strengthen action in improving opportunities and promoting youth-friendly and youth-safe environments, all underpinned by the voice of young people in designing and implementing local recreation policies and plans. Most importantly, the policy stresses and supports the view that young people have the desire *and* the potential to be active participants in the local community and in society generally. They want to be part of what's happening and to have their views and ways of enjoying themselves considered a positive aspect of community life.

Very much in keeping with the new Programme for Government, I believe that this policy represents a great opportunity to support and strengthen young people and their communities, engendering mutual respect and enriching young people's experiences of growing up.

Brendan Smith, TD
Minister for Children
September 2007

Acknowledgements

Message from Sylda Langford
Director General, Office of the Minister for Children

I know that young people have been keenly awaiting the publication of the National Recreation Policy and I would like to thank several people who have been instrumental in bringing the policy document to fruition.

First and foremost, I would like to explicitly acknowledge the wonderful support and enthusiastic cooperation received from the young people, aged 12 to 18, who actively participated in the research and the public consultation, supported by their parents and teachers.

We are also greatly indebted to Dr. Áine de Róiste and Ms. Joan Dinneen, Department of Social and General Studies, Cork Institute of Technology, who conducted and facilitated the research, and to Ms. Sandra Roe who compiled the report on the public consultation on behalf of the Office of the Minister for Children. Their reports provided valuable information on a range of issues relating to young people and contributed significantly to the development of the policy.

Finally, I would like to record our deep appreciation to the Steering Group, chaired by Ms. Mary Golden, Office of the Minister for Children, and comprising representatives of those Government departments and agencies involved in the provision of services and programmes for young people, who had responsibility for overseeing the development of the policy.

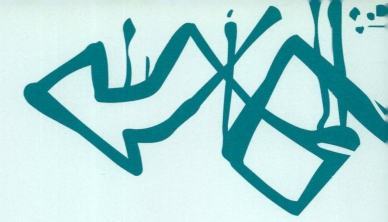

The issue of recreation is being addressed by Government to meet commitments made in the United Nations Convention on the Rights of the Child (UN, 1989), the National Children's Strategy (Department of Health and Children, 2000a) and the Agreed Programme for Government (Government of Ireland, 2002). The overall objective of the National Recreation Policy is to provide appropriate publicly funded recreational opportunities for young people between the ages of 12 and 18. The policy also aims to provide strategic direction to Government departments, local authorities, City and County Development Boards, the youth sector, the community and voluntary sectors, and other interested parties to develop recreational opportunities for young people in an informed and appropriate manner.

Background

The original impetus for addressing recreation came from young people themselves during the consultation process for the development of the National Children's Strategy, which was published in November 2000. The absence of leisure and recreational facilities and activities for children and young people was the most pressing issue raised in the course of the consultations. Under the National Children's Strategy, the Government included a commitment to develop national play and recreation policies to enrich the lives of children and to provide them with experiences and competencies that would serve them well in later life. The Programme for Government (June 2002) built on that commitment, stating that: *'We will develop a National Play and Recreation Policy which will aim to ensure that all children have access to at least a minimum standard of play and recreation facilities.'*

The National Play Policy, *Ready, Steady, Play!* was published by Government in 2004 to address the needs of younger children, particularly of primary school age (NCO, 2004). The Government is now addressing the needs of young people between the ages of 12 and 18 by developing the National Recreation Policy.

Developing the policy

The process of developing the National Recreation Policy was informed through research commissioned by the Office of the Minister for Children (OMC). The aims of the research were to determine what young Irish people do in their free time and what are the barriers and supports they experience and their aspirations with regard to recreation and leisure. Research was undertaken in 2004 with over 2,260 young people, aged 12-18, across a random sample of 51 schools throughout the country (De Róiste and Dinneen, 2005). Focus groups were also held to gain insight into the additional needs of young people with disabilities and those at a socio-economic disadvantage.

In addition, a consultation document was published in May 2005 which set out the reasons for developing the policy, as well as the principles and objectives that were considered necessary to underpin its development (NCO, 2005a). A public consultation was then conducted, the purpose of which was to gather views, comments and suggestions for the development of the policy based on the consultation document (NCO, 2006). Overall, 940 people responded to the public consultation, with three-quarters of all respondents being under the age of 18 years.

The findings of the research and the key issues emerging from the public consultation were considered in the context of the development of the National Recreation Policy.

Policy objectives

For the purpose of the National Recreation Policy, recreation is defined as *'comprising all positive activities in which a person may choose to take part that will make his or her leisure time more interesting, more enjoyable and personally satisfying'*.

The policy aims to encompass both organised activities for young people as well as more casual activities that young people engage in during their free time.

Seven core objectives have been set for the policy, as follows:

1. Give young people a voice in the design, implementation and monitoring of recreation policies and facilities.
2. Promote organised activities for young people and examine ways to motivate them to be involved.
3. Ensure that the recreational needs of young people are met through the development of youth-friendly and safe environments.
4. Maximise the range of recreational opportunities available for young people who are marginalised, disadvantaged or who have a disability.
5. Promote relevant qualifications/standards in the provision of recreational activities.
6. Develop a partnership approach in developing and funding recreational opportunities across the statutory, community and voluntary sectors.
7. Improve information on, evaluation and monitoring of recreational provision for young people in Ireland.

Recommendations to address key issues under each of these objectives, and responsibility for achieving them, are clearly defined in an Implementation Action Plan (*see Chapter 11*).

Structure of the policy

Chapter 1 sets out the context for developing the National Recreation Policy for young people, outlining the background to the impetus for addressing recreation and the importance of recreation in young people's lives.

Chapter 2 describes the barriers and motivators to participation in recreation by young people, including those with special needs.

Chapter 3 sets forth the principles and objectives underpinning the policy and links to other strategies and policies.

Chapter 4 examines Objective 1 of the policy and the benefits of promoting the active involvement and engagement of young people in the design and implementation of recreation policies and facilities.

Chapter 5 focuses on Objective 2, exploring the range of organised activities that young people engage in and ways in which to promote and encourage their involvement in recreational pursuits.

Chapter 6 reviews Objective 3, examining the casual activities of young people and issues around the wider physical environment in which they participate in recreation, including outdoor facilities.

Chapter 7 focuses on Objective 4 and issues surrounding accessibility to recreation by young people who have special needs, such as those who are marginalised, disadvantaged or who have a disability.

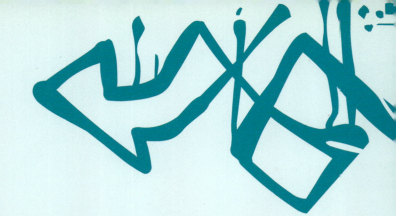

Chapter 8 examines Objective 5 and standards in relation to the quality and safety of recreational facilities used by young people, as well as issues about the qualifications of people dealing with young people in recreational settings.

Chapter 9 concentrates on Objective 6, identifying the role of Government departments and agencies in the provision of recreational facilities and programmes for young people, together with measures for developing a partnership approach across the statutory, community and voluntary sectors to improve coordination at national and local level.

Chapter 10 identifies the measures proposed under Objective 7 to improve the dissemination of information to young people on the range of facilities available.

Chapter 11 describes the administrative framework to drive forward and oversee the implementation of the National Recreation Policy, together with details of the Implementation Action Plan in which the responsibilities and timescales are set out for the achievement of targeted actions under the seven objectives of the policy.

Appendix 1 provides details of the role of each Government department and agency involved in the development and implementation of the National Recreation Policy.

Appendix 2 sets out the membership of the Steering Group overseeing development of the policy.

chapter one

The context for developing a recreation policy for young people

Vision:

'An Ireland where the importance of recreation is recognised so that young people experience a range of quality recreational opportunities to enrich their lives and promote physical, cultural, mental and social well-being' (NCO, 2005a)

The primary objective of the National Recreation Policy is to provide appropriate, publicly funded recreational opportunities for young people between the ages of 12 and 18. The policy also aims to provide strategic direction to Government departments, local authorities, City and County Development Boards, the youth sector, the community and voluntary sectors, and other interested parties to develop recreational opportunities for young people in an informed and appropriate manner. The policy has a 10-year timeframe.

The issue of recreation is being addressed by the Government to meet commitments in the United Nations Convention on the Rights of the Child (UN, 1989), the National Children's Strategy (Department of Health and Children, 2000a) and the Agreed Programme for Government (Government of Ireland, 2002).

The UN Convention on the Rights of the Child was ratified by Ireland in 1992. Article 31 of the Convention recognises *the right of the child to rest and leisure, to engage in play and recreational activities appropriate to the age of the child and to participate freely in cultural life and the arts*.

The National Children's Strategy, *Our Children — Their Lives*, published by the Department of Health and Children (2000a), specifically refers to the issue of play and recreation in its Objective D, which states that *children will have access to play, sport, recreation and cultural activities to enrich their experience of childhood*. The lack of play and recreational facilities was identified by children themselves in the consultation process that preceded the National Children's Strategy (Department of Health and Children, 2000b).

The commitment to a National Recreation Policy was reinforced in the Programme for Government in 2002, which stated *We will develop a National Play and Recreation Policy which will aim to ensure that all children have access to at least a minimum standard of play and recreation facilities*. The National Play Policy, *Ready, Steady, Play!* was published by Government in 2004 (NCO, 2004). It was designed primarily for children of primary school age. The Government is now addressing the needs of teenagers through the National Recreation Policy.

This chapter sets out the reasons for developing the National Recreation Policy, the benefits of recreation for young people and the wider social and economic context in which young people engage in recreation.

Background

As with the National Play Policy, the impetus for addressing recreation came from young people themselves during the consultation process on the National Children's Strategy. Young people identified more leisure and recreational facilities and activities as the most pressing issue in the public consultation for the strategy (Department of Health and Children, 2000b). Recreation and facilities for young people have been raised by young people at almost every Dáil na nÓg (Youth Parliament) since its inception in 2001.

While young people have identified a lack of facilities as a significant 'quality of life' issue for them, there has been considerable public investment in sporting and recreational facilities in recent years, although this is not exclusively targeted at young people. The Sports Capital Programme, for example, provides National Lottery funding towards the development of local, regional and national facilities. In the period 1998-2005, a total of €395 million was allocated under the Sports Capital Programme to 4,923 projects nationwide across a range of sports and to a variety of voluntary and community organisations, including sports clubs. This funding has provided badly needed investment in sports facilities, varying from small local sports clubs to regional and national sports centres, including a number of municipal sports centres developed by local authorities. In addition, there has been expenditure by the Irish Sports Council since its establishment in 1999 in providing opportunities for young people to participate in sport and recreation — particularly the provision of €32.5 million in funding to the three main field sports (GAA, FAI, IRFU) during 2001-2005 to assist in increasing participation by young people and improving standards in the area of underage sports.

The Government is committed to developing additional public swimming pool facilities. €93 million has been allocated for this purpose under the current round of the Sports Capital Programme between 2000 and April 2006. This represents the most sustained attempt to improve the stock of local public swimming pools since the early 1970s.

Since 1999, through the investment in the Cardiovascular Health Strategy, the Health Service Executive (HSE) now has Physical Activity Coordinators in place throughout the country who are working in partnership at regional and local level to increase physical activity levels across all age groups. The HSE has also supported the piloting and development of youth cafés in a number of cities and towns.

The Department of Community, Rural and Gaeltacht Affairs has allocated €106 million under the Young People's Facilities and Services Fund to assist in the development of facilities (including sports and recreational) and services for youth at risk in areas of disadvantage, where a significant drug problem exists or has the potential to develop. The Department also has responsibility for RAPID (Revitalising Areas by Planning Investment and Development), the Dormant Accounts Fund, the CLÁR (Ceantair Laga Árd-Riachtanais) Programme and a range of other volunteering and philanthropic initiatives.

The Department of Education and Science has provided €198 million towards the provision of youth work programmes and services in the period 2001-2006.

Funding of €2 million has also been provided by the Department of the Environment, Heritage and Local Government in 2005 towards the provision of 21 skateboard parks throughout the country. €10.1 million has also been put into public play facilities since 2004. This is in addition to the substantial commitment and ongoing funding by local authorities to the development of play and recreational facilities locally.

Despite this substantial public investment, it is clear that existing programmes and facilities are not meeting all the needs of young people. As indicated above, while there has been substantial investment in public swimming pools, there remain issues about access to them, particularly in rural areas. Other publicly funded outdoor facilities for teenagers, such as skateboard parks, are developing from a very low base.

Many young people want an alternative to traditional recreation such as sport. In research commissioned for the development of this policy, 59% of young people believed that there was very little leisure provision for teenagers in their locality (De Róiste and Dinneen, 2005). Young people identified, in particular, the need for casual recreational opportunities, such as drop-in centres and youth cafés. There was also a very strong view among young people that they should be consulted about recreation programmes and facilities, and that they should be involved in the governance arrangements put in place.

Defining recreation

For the purpose of the National Recreation Policy, recreation is defined as '*comprising all positive activities in which a person may choose to take part that will make his or her leisure time more interesting, more enjoyable and personally satisfying*' (adapted from Laidlaw Foundation, 2001).

This policy aims to encompass both organised activities for young people as well as the more casual activities that young people engage in during their free time. Recreation can include reading, recreational sport, art, music in a group, 'hanging out', camping, surfing the Net and many more activities. Recreation can be distinguished from organised sport because it does not necessarily involve competition; it is subject to the starting and stopping wishes of the individual and is less constrained by rules. However, many activities that would normally be thought of as sport if they are done informally and non-competitively can be viewed as recreation (Smith and Therberge, 1987). The Irish Sports Council Act, 1999 supports this idea by defining recreational sport as '*all forms of physical activity which, through casual or regular participation, aim at expressing or improving physical fitness and mental well-being and at forming social relationships*' (Government of Ireland, 1999a).

Importance of recreation in young people's lives

What young people do in their free time is a very important part of growing up. Adolescence is a formative transitional period from childhood to adulthood (Hamburg and Takanishi, 1989). It is a time when young people form their identity and undergo major adjustments to changes within themselves and in society as altered expectations are placed on them. Great importance is attached to peer groups and cliques, which are 'almost always held together by shared interests, tastes, activities, and/or hobbies' (Thurlow, 2002). Adolescence is a time of exploring and making commitments in interpersonal relationships in the four domains of friendship, dating, sex roles and recreation; this exploratory period is an important time for the development of identity (Grotevant *et al*, 1982).

How young people spend their free time has a major impact on their development, socialisation and future life. Leisure provides the opportunity for young people to gain control over their attention processes, acquire critical adult skills and become integrated into their communities (Larson and Verma, 1999). The World Health Organization emphasises the importance of leisure-time activities (WHO, 2002): it sees participation in varied forms of activity as giving young people opportunities for self-expression, feelings of autonomy and achievement. These positive effects can also help to counteract risks and harm caused by demanding, competitive, stressful and sedentary lifestyles. Involvement in activities such as sport, arts, music and hobbies can foster the adoption of other healthy behaviour, including the avoidance of tobacco, alcohol, drugs and aggression.

Policy for all young people

In line with the principles underpinning the National Children's Strategy, the National Recreation Policy is for *all* young people.

Young people between the ages of 12 and 18 are not a homogeneous group. There are differences in recreational activities engaged in by boys and girls, who also experience different barriers and motivators to participation in recreation. There are also differences in the activities undertaken between different age groups. A Scottish study of young people's leisure and lifestyles found that leisure focus through the adolescent years initially shows a strong reliance by the young adolescent on adult-organised clubs and activities (Hendry *et al*, 1993). The next phase of an adolescent's leisure development shows a move towards casual leisure and the final stage is a move towards more commercially organised leisure. These findings are confirmed in the Waterford study by Connor (2003), entitled *The sporting, leisure and lifestyle patterns of Irish adolescents*, and in the national research undertaken for the development of this policy (De Róiste and Dinneen, 2005). Even within the same activity, efforts must be made to ensure that what is being provided is age-appropriate. Also, different issues arise for young people living in urban and rural areas. For example, research has found that young people in rural areas are more likely to experience difficulties with transport than those in urban areas (De Róiste and Dinneen, 2005). Particular difficulties in accessing recreation are experienced by young people from minority groups, including young people with disabilities, early school-leavers and young people from the Traveller community. All of these issues need to be taken into account in developing recreational opportunities for young people.

Whole Child Perspective

The development of the National Recreation Policy for Young People has been underpinned by the concept of the 'whole child perspective'. This concept was first set out in the National Children's Strategy in 2000 and provides a broad conceptual underpinning for developments around children's lives. The 'whole child perspective' facilitates an approach to children's lives that is holistic, child-centred and integrated. In addition, importantly, it takes account of the fact that children themselves have the capacity to shape their own lives and the lives of those around them, while at the same time being shaped by the formal and informal context within which they live.

As stated in the National Children's Strategy, the purpose of the whole child perspective is '*to provide a common framework for all stakeholders involved in children's lives to discuss, plan and develop ways in which children and young people can reach their potential*'.

The whole child perspective is underpinned by an assumption that children and young people are active participants in their own lives and that they are entitled to a voice in matters that affect them. This is reflected in the objectives set out in this policy.

Components of the whole child perspective

The whole child perspective comprises three broad domains, with interlinkages between and within them. These three domains are:
1. children's innate capacity;
2. children's relationships;
3. formal and informal supports.

1. Children's innate capacity

This domain sets out nine dimensions that can be used to identify outcomes which children achieve at each stage of their development and which eventually provide the capacity for coping with adulthood:
- physical and mental well-being;
- emotional and behavioural well-being;
- intellectual capacity;
- spiritual and moral well-being;
- identity;
- self-care skills;
- family relationships;
- social and peer relationships;
- social presentation.

It is important that each of these dimensions is fostered and supported. Equally important is the recognition that any individual dimension can have an impact on others. There is strong evidence, for example, that girls become less interested in sports as they go through their teenage years and this is a normal progression of their development. If they do not take up an alternative physical activity, it is likely that their physical well-being and development will be compromised. In addition, however, because they are not involved in sports they may discontinue friendships and relationships developed through sports organisations. This may have consequences for their development around the dimension of social relationships. It is important, therefore, to recognise that all dimensions of children's innate capacity have the potential to influence each other and this must be taken into account when looking at how their recreational needs can be supported.

2. Children's relationships

This domain sets out the complex set of relationships that are recognised as essential for a satisfying and successful childhood. These relationships range from the family, the primary source of care, all the way up to the State, which acts as the ultimate guarantor of their rights. The importance of relationships at every level is recognised within the whole child perspective — peer relationships, relationships between young people and their communities, relationships required for local coordination of facilities and the use of a partnership approach to developments.

3. Formal and informal supports

This domain includes essential supports and services to be provided for children, firstly, through the informal supports of the primary social networks of family, extended family and community, and, secondly, through the formal supports provided by the voluntary sector, commercial sector, the State and its agencies. Both types of supports provide the conduit through which children draw the support and services they need and from which they benefit.

The holistic nature of the whole child perspective leads to a recognition that while each of the three domains set out above are important in their own right, it is only by taking account of the inter- and intra-domain relationships that a full and comprehensive understanding of children's lives can be achieved.

In planning recreational opportunities for young people, this policy will recognise and encourage all stakeholders to consider how the provision of formal and informal supports (such as facilities and equipment), mediated through relationships (including parents, service providers and volunteers), can impact on children's development across some or all of the nine dimensions outlined above.

Benefits of recreation for young people

Driver (1992) identifies six ways in which people benefit from recreation:

- **physiological benefits**, including reduced incidence of disease and increased sense of wellness;
- **psycho-physiological benefits**, including reduction of tension and anxiety, and improved sense of well-being;
- **psychological benefits**, including improved sense of self-esteem, freedom and independence, improved problem-solving capabilities and enhanced perception of quality of life;
- **social/cultural benefits**, including pride in one's community, cultural and historical awareness, and increased family bonds;
- **environmental benefits**, including awareness of the need to protect the environment and to maintain outdoor recreational sites, as well as protecting cultural, historical and heritage sites;
- **economic benefits**, including opportunities for employment in the leisure industry, which is one of the largest industries in the world in terms of employment and income generation.

Leisure and recreational activities can also facilitate a number of developmental processes in adolescence (Dworkin *et al*, 2003). These include the development of identity, self-concept and self-knowledge, the development of initiative, the development of emotional competencies, the formation of new connections with peers and knowledge of peers, the development of social skills, learning to work with others, leadership skills and the acquirement of social capital.

Social capital

In its 2003 report on *The Policy Implications of Social Capital*, the National Economic and Social Forum (NESF) describes social capital as '*important social processes and relationships — informal social support networks, friendship, neighbourhood generosity, interpersonal trust and volunteering activity — but also aspects of local and community development, public-private voluntary partnerships and civic spirit*' (NESF, 2003).

The report indicates that Ireland is rated as average, or above average, in European comparisons on most indicators of social capital. The report concludes that sport and recreation play a very important role in relation to social capital, particularly in regard to the dominant role of sport in volunteering and organisational membership. The importance of sport in the generation of social capital in Ireland is reiterated by Ruddle and Mulvihill (1999).

Organised recreational activity outside of sport is also heavily dependent on the contribution of community-minded individuals who commit their time to clubs, summer projects and other activities. There are over 40,000 adult leaders involved in the youth work sector. There is also a significant commitment by teachers to young people's recreational opportunities after school hours.

The contribution of young people themselves to the development of recreation programmes and as active citizens in their own community will also be highlighted in this report.

Developing the policy

A two-strand approach was taken to developing the National Recreation Policy. The first involved research being commissioned by the Office of the Minister for Children (then the National Children's Office) to examine young people's views on the opportunities, barriers and supports to recreation and leisure. This research was undertaken in November 2004, with over 2,260 young people, aged 12-18, taking part through a random sample of 51 schools across the country. As part of the study, focus groups were also held to gain insight into the additional needs of young people from minority groups, including early school-leavers, young people with disabilities and young Travellers. The findings from this research were published in 2005 and provide a picture of leisure practices and preferences of young Irish people, as well as identifying the main barriers and supports to their participation in recreation (De Róiste and Dinneen, 2005).

The second approach to developing the policy involved the production of a consultation document, setting out the principles and objectives of the proposed National Recreation Policy (NCO, 2005a). A public consultation was then held to gather views, comments and suggestions for the development of the policy. In addition, responses were sought on the following issues:
- the main barriers and motivators to participation in recreation;
- the single biggest need in regard to recreation for young people;
- the key issues that need to be addressed in developing and funding recreational opportunities for young people;
- examples of recreation projects and programmes for young people that have worked well.

Overall, 940 people responded to the public consultation. Of these, 457 respondents (50%) were aged 15-17, while 222 (25%) were aged 18 or over; 43% of respondents were male and 57% were female. There was a good geographical spread of respondents, with at least one person from each of the 26 counties. The report of the public consultation was published in 2006 (NCO, 2006).

The development of the National Recreation Policy was overseen by a Steering Group, chaired by the Office of the Minister for Children and included representatives of the Department of Health and Children; the Health Service Executive; the Department of the Environment, Heritage and Local Government and the local authorities; the Department of Community, Rural and Gaeltacht Affairs; the Department of Arts, Sport and Tourism; the Irish Sports Council; the Department of Education and Science; the Department of Justice, Equality and Law Reform; and the Department of Communications, Marine and Natural Reources. Membership of the Steering Group is set out in Appendix 2.

Context in which young people engage in recreation

Demography

Ireland's population has increased by 12.3% to over 4 million in the period between 1995 and 2004. This was the second highest rate of increase in the European Union (EU) and was significantly higher than the EU25's growth of just 2.2%. Ireland has the second highest proportion of population aged 0-14 years in the EU, second only to Iceland (Eurostat, 2005). There are an estimated 1.01 million children under the age of 18 years living in Ireland (CSO, 2003), of which 358,381 are young people aged 12-17. This age group accounts for 9.15% of the population. The percentage of young people in this age group is mapped out by county in Figure 1.

Figure 1: Number of 12-17 year-olds as % of national population, by county (2006)

Education and employment

Education has become more important in the lives of young people, with more school-leavers attending third-level education than ever before. The proportion of people aged 25-34 in Ireland with third-level education rose from 27.1% in 1999 to 39.4% in 2004 (CSO, 2004a and 2006).

It is becoming increasingly common for young people to be involved in education and in employment simultaneously. There is a clear rise in the proportion of those working part-time across the teenage years, reaching a peak in Transition Year. This has implications for the amount of free time at their disposal and for how they might choose to use it (Department of Education and Science, 2003a). More young people are now engaging in part-time work to finance their 'lifestyle' rather than because of a financial need and also because it gives them feelings of independence (McCoy and Smyth, 2004).

Growth of population centres

The growth in employment and rising house prices, particularly in the Dublin area, has resulted in the rapid expansion of towns and villages within commuting distance of Dublin. The populations of Kildare and Meath have increased by over one-fifth between 1996 and 2002. Increases in the population of Westmeath (13.5%), Wexford (11.7%), Laois (11%), Louth (10.5%) and Carlow (10.6%) reflect to some extent the widening of the Dublin commuter belt beyond Meath, Kildare and Wicklow (CSO, 2003). Much of this development has taken place without putting in place the necessary infrastructure to support play and recreational facilities for children and young people.

This trend is expected to continue. For example, the population of the Greater Dublin Area (i.e. Dublin, Kildare, Meath and Wicklow) is projected to increase by over 500,000 people by 2021. The CSO has projected that the fastest growing areas of the country will be the Mid-East (Kildare, Meath and Wicklow) and the West (Galway City and counties Mayo and Roscommon). The young population (0-14 years) will increase in all regions between 2002 and 2021. Consequently, it is important to devise a strategic approach to the development of recreation and leisure services so as to ensure that young people in these new urban centres have access to positive recreational opportunities.

The urban landscape is also changing with the introduction of high-density housing. This has implications for the environment in which children and young people engage in play and recreation.

Cultural diversity

Ireland is becoming an increasingly multicultural society and the make-up of the youth population is more culturally varied than ever before. As a result, young people in Ireland are growing into adulthood in a much more culturally diverse environment than was formerly the case (Department of Education and Science, 2003a). There are 61,778 young people under the age of 19 living in Ireland who are non-nationals (CSO, 2002). There are also 10,000 Travellers aged 0-14 years and 4,850 Travellers aged 15-24 living in Ireland (CSO, 2004b).

Recreation, therefore, needs to cater for the diverse needs of young people from all cultures. It can help to integrate young people from ethnic minorities into Irish society, as well as facilitate contact between young people from different cultures. This can help to challenge racist attitudes and enable young people to get to know each other as individuals rather than as members of a particular group (McCrea, 2003).

Rise in consumerism

We live in an increasingly consumer society. Ireland has the greatest penetration of Sony Play Stations in the world after Japan (Department of Health and Children, 2000a). People, and particularly perhaps the young, are encouraged to see themselves as making autonomous individual decisions about, for example, what to buy, what to wear, what to listen to, what to read or watch, where to spend their leisure time and what types of relationship to have (Department of Education and Science, 2003a). Advertising can harm young people by making them feel inadequate if they are unable to keep up with the latest products (Cohn, 2000). The culture of consumerism may have particularly adverse effects on disadvantaged children by creating needs that go unmet (Byrne *et al*, 2006).

Challenges for young people's well-being

There are increasing pressures on Ireland's young population due in part to rapid social change. One manifestation of this is the number of suicides. In 2003, there were 444 reported suicides, with 108 in the 15-24 age category. Overall, males represented 81% of suicides, while females represented 19% (*see* www.cso.ie). The rate of youth suicide in Ireland is currently the 5th highest in the EU, at 15.7 per 100,000 for 15-24 year-olds (HSE, 2005). The 2005 report *Reach Out: National Strategy for Action on Suicide Prevention 2005-2014* contains a recommendation for the provision of increased community, sports and leisure facilities in county development plans (HSE, 2005). Physical activity among teenagers is associated with good mental health and is related to higher levels of self-esteem, as well as lower levels of perceived stress and anxiety (Calfas *et al*, 1994). These findings are further explored in Chapter 5.

How recreation is changing

Technology

Recreation for young people has become increasingly based on technology. Technology-orientated recreation (such as watching television, playing computer games and surfing the Internet) are popular activities among young Irish people (Connor, 2003; De Róiste and Dinneen, 2005; Fahey *et al*, 2005). Research undertaken for the purpose of developing this policy found that over 70% of the young people sampled watch television every day, almost 95% have mobile phones and over one-third play computer games every day, although this latter activity was more popular with boys than with girls (De Róiste and Dinneen, 2005).

While the new media technologies offer enormous opportunities, it is also the case that important information and communication is by-passing the normal gate-keepers (i.e. parents) via mobiles, television, Internet, etc. and penetrating the protection that young people should have at this stage of their development (Ballymun Partnership, 2005).

Shopping

Shopping is a popular recreational activity for many young people, especially girls. Girls strongly 'peer orientate' or form and maintain friendship groups or cliques on the basis of a shared appreciation of clothes as well as music and personal qualities. This may be one factor explaining girls' high frequency in

this activity (Thurlow, 2002). Boys, on the other hand, 'peer orientate' primarily on the basis of a shared interest in sport and/or computers (Thurlow, 2002; Youniss *et al*, 1994). These findings are supported by the research carried out for this policy, which found that shopping is a popular leisure-time activity for girls (De Róiste and Dinneen, 2005). Looking at shops was valued by young girls for a number of reasons, including '*it's great to see new clothes*', '*we like thinking about how to spend money*', '*it's fun with your friends*' and '*it's in the city*'.

The environment

Environment and 'places to go' have been identified as indicators of well-being among young people. A young person's environment is 'an important area for child well-being' (Hanafin and Brooks, 2005). The environment is very significant for young people in terms of the time they spend 'hanging out' with their friends or going to and from activities. The overwhelming majority of young people (93%) in the research carried out for the development of this policy said that they like hanging out with their friends in their free time, with 61% reporting hanging out every day or most days (De Róiste and Dinneen, 2005). A number of studies have highlighted adults' perceptions of teenagers hanging out on the streets or in public spaces as a potential threat to public order (Valentine *et al*, 1998). Young people see themselves as being 'hassled' when hanging out in groups, partly because of their high visibility (Devlin, 2006).

It is important that young people are visible in their local community. While this policy looks at the issue of providing young people with alternatives to hanging around outside, the legitimacy of young people's presence in public places needs to be recognised, provided they are not engaged in anti-social behaviour.

Safe environments are also an increasingly important issue for young people. Only two-thirds of young people in the research for this policy reported feeling safe going to and from activities in the evening time (De Róiste and Dinneen, 2005). Safety was a much more significant issue for girls than for boys. Adequate lighting and footpaths, especially in rural areas, also emerged as a safety issue among young people in the public consultation.

The physical environment can also affect levels of physical activity. Young people in low-income areas have reported that neighbourhood safety is important for physical activity (Sallis *et al*, 1996). The frequency of physical activity was associated with the perception of 'safe adults' (meaning trustworthy) at facilities and safe areas for facilities. Young people who reported busy traffic on the roads near their home were less likely to view their area as a safe place to walk after dark or as a safe place for children to play outside (Woods *et al*, 2005). These findings are further explored in Chapter 6.

Alcohol and drug use

There are aspects of young people's leisure-time activity that give cause for concern, according to a report by the Health Promotion Unit (Department of Health and Children, 2003). Findings show that 29% of young Irish people under 18 reported drinking alcohol in the last month. More boys (34%) reported being current drinkers than girls (24%). More risky alcohol consumption increases with age and boys (35%) are more likely to engage in this behaviour than girls (24%). The proportion of Irish students who drank any alcohol during the last 12 months is a little higher than the European average — 88% compared to 83%. However, the proportion that had been drunk during the same period is substantially higher than the European average — 72% compared to 53% (ESPAD, 2003). This, in turn, can lead to anti-social behaviour. The largest number of offences (20%) committed by young offenders are alcohol-related (Department of Justice, Equality and Law Reform, 2005b).

The use of marijuana by young people is twice as common in Ireland than the average for all European countries (39% versus 21%), while the use of illicit drugs other than marijuana is only slightly above average (9% versus 6%). Use of inhalants, however, is about twice the European average (18% compared to 10%) (ESPAD, 2003).

Providing attractive alcohol-free and drug-free alternative venues for young people can form part of the solution to underage drinking and drug-taking when combined with other policy measures. Young people have identified that having somewhere safe to go at night and at weekends can reduce the amount of anti-social behaviour (see also Chapter 6).

Decline in physical activity

Research over the years shows a decline in physical activity, particularly among teenage girls (Centre for Health Promotion Studies, 2003). Between 1998 and 2002, girls aged 12-14 changed their physical activity levels significantly: vigorous activity decreased for this age group from 49% in 1998 to 44% in 2002. While activity levels are known to decrease with age, this finding shows the drop is occurring at a younger age. There were also significant increases in the reported levels of no physical activity and physical activity less than once a week between 1998 and 2002.

The 2005 report entitled *Take Part* (Physical Activity Research for Teenagers) found that 56% of participants were not involved in moderate or vigorous physical exercise for more than four days a week or at least 60 minutes per day, while some 80% were not regularly active for more than five days (Woods *et al*, 2005). Girls were significantly less likely to be physically active and had a lower level of aerobic fitness compared with a similar age group in Northern Ireland (Boreham and Riddoch, 2001).

Participation in recreational activity, including recreational sport as well as dance and drama, can form part of the solution in tackling the risks and harm associated with sedentary lifestyles (see also Chapter 5).

Traditional recreation activities

While recreation and the environment in which young people participate in recreation is changing, young people in Ireland are still engaged in a wide range of traditional recreational activities. These include sports, clubs, reading, volunteering and taking care of pets.

Involvement in sport

Research commissioned for the development of this policy found that 88% of young people report playing at least one sport (De Róiste and Dinneen, 2005). More boys (91%) play sport than girls (86%). Soccer, Gaelic football and hurling are the most popular sports for boys, while basketball, Gaelic football and swimming are the most popular sports for girls. There are, however, marked gender differences in terms of the frequency of participation, with almost two-thirds of boys taking part twice a week or more compared to 40% of girls, and one-third of boys taking part four or more times a week compared to 10% of girls (Fahey *et al*, 2005). These findings are further explored in Chapter 5.

Involvement in clubs

Almost 80% of Irish secondary school children participate in sports played in clubs. The most popular clubs for boys are soccer, Gaelic football, hurling and rugby clubs, while Gaelic football, dance, soccer, camogie and swimming clubs are the most popular for girls (Fahey *et al*, 2005). Research commissioned

for the development of this policy found that almost 20% of young people are members of youth clubs and 10% are members of the Scouts or Guides, with slightly more boys than girls as members (De Róiste and Dinneen, 2005). Choir or folk groups are also popular with young people, with 26% reporting to be members. Again, there are marked gender differences: significantly more girls are members of choir or folk groups than boys, with 38% of girls reporting membership compared to 9% of boys. Drama emerged as a popular hobby, with 9% of young people reporting participation in clubs or at school.

Reading

Reading is still popular, although it tends to be more popular among teenage girls than teenage boys. Recent research found that over half of the young people sampled read in their free time every day or most days (De Róiste and Dinneen, 2005). Girls read significantly more than boys, and young people from higher socio-economic backgrounds have a higher reading frequency.

Volunteering

In the research undertaken for this policy, just under 4% of young people reported taking part in voluntary work (De Róiste and Dinneen, 2005). Slightly more girls participated than boys, and young people attending rural schools participated more in community and charity groups than those attending urban schools. Voluntary work also emerged in the public consultation as an example of recreation for young people which works well. Specific examples given included Foróige volunteering projects, Special Olympics clubs and the Best Buddies Programme.

Pets

Looking after pets has been identified as an important indicator of well-being among young people and pets can play a significant role in the lives of children — *'The role of animals/pets is one which should not be underestimated as in some cases the response from the pet may be the only consistent, loving unconditional response the child has access to'* (Hanafin and Brooks, 2005, p. 60). The importance of pets is supported by the research carried out for this policy. Taking care of pets was reported as the second most popular hobby among young people: 22% regarded it as their favourite hobby, especially among 12-13 year-old boys (De Róiste and Dinneen, 2005).

Summary

Irish teenagers are growing up in a period of rapid social change and in an increasingly culturally diverse environment. They are engaged in a wide range of leisure and recreational activities, ranging from the use of new technology to more traditional activities such as sport and looking after pets, as well as more risky activities such as drinking and drug-taking.

Positive recreational opportunities can make an important contribution to young people's development and can help to counteract the risks and harm associated with sedentary lifestyles and risky behaviour. While there has been substantial investment in facilities in recent years, this is not meeting the needs of all young people, particularly those who do not participate in sport. This National Recreation Policy seeks to address this and other issues emerging from the research and the public consultation. It also looks at the contribution that young people themselves can make to developing their own recreational opportunities and as active citizens in their own right.

chapter two

Barriers and motivators to participation in recreation

There are a number of barriers and motivators that can either hinder or encourage participation in recreational activities among young people.

Intrapersonal constraints

Intrapersonal constraints are individual characteristics, traits and beliefs that encourage or enhance participation in leisure (Crawford *et al*, 1991). They include enjoyment, competition, self-confidence, body image, shyness and friends. These constraints are significant from a policy perspective because there may be a sub-group of young people who are unable to negotiate their way through them and who, without positive intervention, may not participate in recreation.

The research carried out for this policy found that young people do what they do because they enjoy it, they want to have fun and they choose to do what is important to them (De Róiste and Dinneen, 2005). In general, there was a high level of intrinsic motivation among the young people surveyed.

Key findings were:
- Enjoyment was a key motivator to positive use of leisure time.
- Competition can be a motivator or a barrier depending on the individual's personality. Boys were more likely to see competition as a motivator than girls.
- Body image is a significant issue for teenage girls. While over 65% of the sample were happy with the way they looked, just over half of these were girls. Research has shown that body image and ideal body size can act as a motivator for girls and young women to exercise (Ingledew and Sullivan, 2002; Tiggerman, 2001). Other research has found negative body image to be a barrier to recreation and in particular to physical activity in young women (Hendry *et al*, 1993; North Western Health Board, 2004).
- There is a strong link between shyness and low motivation for leisure activities. A small (6%) but significant number of young people sampled scored low on leisure motivation. This group participate little in sports, hobbies or groups, and may be in need of more targeted intervention to encourage participation.

The public consultation identified friends, enjoyment and keeping fit as key motivators to participation in recreation. Intrapersonal barriers included lack of interest, shyness, self-consciousness and lack of skill.

Interpersonal constraints

Interpersonal constraints are the result of interpersonal interaction. For example, an interpersonal barrier would be an inability to find a partner or a group of friends with whom to engage in a desired leisure activity or it could denote someone who receives no family or peer support (De Róiste and Dinneen, 2005). Examples of interpersonal motivators would be parental permission and family encouragement.

The research undertaken for this policy found that young Irish people appear to be well supported with regard to leisure, particularly in the early teenage years (De Róiste and Dinneen, 2005). Parental support, and to a lesser extent familial support, is high. This is supported by other research, which has highlighted the importance of the family, and the father in particular, for involvement in leisure (Lewko and Greendorfer, 1998). Young people whose parental occupation is professional or managerial are more likely to report familial encouragement than those whose parents are unskilled or on welfare (De Róiste and Dinneen, 2005). Adolescents who felt they received higher family support and higher peer support for involvement in physical activity or sport were significantly more likely to be regularly physically active than children who perceived low social support. In both cases, boys perceived this support more than girls (Woods *et al*, 2005).

The public consultation also identified parents and families, as well as teachers and coaches, as motivators to participation in recreation.

Research carried out for this policy found that less than half of the young people surveyed prefer activities where there is an instructor or a leader (De Róiste and Dinneen, 2005). This finding is significant, particularly in relation to some activities where not liking the leader was a significant reason for dropping out of the activity.

Structural constraints

Structural barriers are physical or material barriers that inhibit participation in recreation. Examples of structural constraints include money, time, homework, transport, safety and the weather. Structural barriers are significant because they are more amenable than some of the other barriers to policy invention.

Key findings from the research undertaken for this policy (De Róiste and Dinneen, 2005) include:

- 59% believe that there is very little leisure provision for adolescents in their locality. Girls report less leisure provision in their area than boys. There is also a significant urban-rural divide. Less than half of city-dwellers, compared to over two-thirds of those who live in the countryside, believe there is very little leisure provision in their area. The lack of recreational facilities and activities also ranked highest in the public consultation. Again, the public consultation found that this was a particular issue for young people from rural areas and that it was a more significant barrier for girls than for boys.
- 15% do not have money to join clubs and activities. Those in the older age groups and the lower socio-economic groups are more likely to experience financial barriers to participation in recreation. Money featured as a significant barrier in the public consultation, particularly when combined with the high cost of commercial recreational activities.
- Time is a barrier to participation in leisure activities and increases dramatically with age, from 31% for 12-year-olds to 71% for 18-year-olds. There are clear gender differences in the amount of time spent doing homework and studying. 43% of girls agree that most of their free time is spent doing homework and studying, as compared to 29% of boys. The differences are striking in Leaving Certificate year, where 60% of the girls sampled agreed that most of their free time is spent studying, while just over one-quarter of boys agreed that this was the case. The public consultation also found that time was a more significant issue for girls than for boys.
- Older teenagers and those in rural areas are more likely to experience difficulties with transport. In the case of older teenagers, this is likely to be due to the broadening of their recreational horizons and because they are more likely to want to be out later at night. The lack of transport was also identified as a barrier in the public consultation. Again, it was a particular issue for young people from rural areas. It was also identified as an issue for younger girls.
- 15% of young people do not feel safe going to and from activities in the evening. This sub-group are most likely to be girls living in urban areas.
- 20% feel that the weather is a barrier to their participation in outdoor activities.

Structural motivators identified in the public consultation included having a good physical education (PE) structure in schools and access to recreational facilities. Overall, structural motivators were the least commonly reported motivator in the public consultation.

Barriers for young people with additional needs

Particular issues arise for young people with additional needs. Structural barriers are the main constraints on leisure experienced by young people from minority groups, such as young people with sensory impairments and physical disabilities, as well as young people from the Traveller community and early school-leavers.

These structural barriers include lack of transport, cost, inadequate equipment, poor access and lack of provision and programming. Several of these difficulties may be experienced at the same time. All pose difficulties that result in a very low level of access to mainstream provision for these minority groups. Dedicated provision also varies greatly across the State. It would appear that Dublin has the best range of leisure provision for young people with disabilities and impairments.

Young people with special needs feel segregated from mainstream leisure activity due to lack of adequate supports and may be confined to leisure activities which are organised through their schools. For some groups, such as young deaf people, the development of new technologies, like mobile phones and the webcam, has been reported to lessen their isolation (Cork Association for the Deaf, 2005). Parental over-protectiveness and geographically spread friendship groups are examples of interpersonal barriers experienced by many young people with disabilities and sensory impairments.

Early school-leavers report little participation in hobbies, sports or clubs. Also of concern is the frequency with which these young people report 'being barred' from various pool halls, cinemas and other venues, leaving them with nothing to do except to hang around.

There is some evidence from the research that young people from the Traveller community are excluded from sports clubs (De Róiste and Dinneen, 2005). Cultural traditions also appear to have a significant effect on the recreation and leisure activities reported by young people from the Traveller community. One notable feature is that female participation in sports and hobbies declines dramatically from the early teenage years (*see Chapter 7*).

The following chapters deal in more detail with the core principles and objectives of the National Recreation Policy, and address the issues identified in the research and public consultation.

chapter three

Principles and objectives underpinning the National Recreation Policy

Principles

Six guiding principles underpin the National Recreation Policy. They are similar to those underpinning the National Play Policy, which was drawn from the consultation process on the National Children's Strategy. They also reflect the values set out in the UN Convention on the Rights of the Child.

These guiding principles are:

- **Centred on young people:** The best interests of young people should be a primary consideration in planning publicly funded recreational opportunities. Young people should be active participants in planning and implementing programmes and facilities, having regard to their age and experience.
- **Family- and community-oriented**: Publicly funded programmes and access to recreational facilities should be established in a manner that supports and empowers families and communities.
- **Equitable**: All young people should have equality of opportunity and access to publicly funded recreation. A key element should be to target investment at communities most in need.
- **Inclusive**: The diversity of young people's experiences, cultures, lifestyles and levels of ability should be recognised in the design and implementation of recreation programmes and facilities.
- **Action-oriented**: Publicly funded recreation programmes and facilities should be focused on achieving specified results to agreed standards in a targeted and cost-effective manner.
- **Integrated:** Recreational facilities and programmes should be delivered in a coordinated manner through integrated needs analysis and policy-planning.

Objectives

Seven objectives have been set for the National Recreation Policy. These objectives reflect a number of changes suggested in the public consultation. In general, the public consultation found a very high level of agreement with the objectives (an average of 96%).

The seven objectives set for this policy are:

1. Give young people a voice in the design, implementation and monitoring of recreation policies and facilities.
2. Promote organised activities for young people and examine ways to motivate them to be involved.
3. Ensure that the recreational needs of young people are met through the development of youth-friendly and safe environments.
4. Maximise the range of recreational opportunities available for young people who are marginalised, disadvantaged or who have a disability.
5. Promote relevant qualifications/standards in the provision of recreational activities.
6. Develop a partnership approach in developing and funding recreational opportunities across the statutory, community and voluntary sectors.
7. Improve information on, evaluation and monitoring of recreational provision for young people in Ireland.

Links to other strategies and policies

The National Recreation Policy links in with the following Government strategies and policies:

- 'Lifecycle framework' under the Social Partnership Agreement, *Towards 2016: Ten-Year Framework Social Partnership Agreement 2006-2015* (2006);
- Ready, Steady, Play! A National Play Policy (2004);
- Irish Sports Council Statement of Strategy 2003-2005 (2003);
- National Health Promotion Strategy 2000-2005 (2000);
- Report of the National Task Force on Obesity (2005);
- Reach Out: National Strategy for Action on Suicide Prevention 2005-2014 (2005);
- Partnership for the Arts: Arts Council Goals 2006-2010 (2005);
- National Youth Work Development Plan 2003-2007 (2003);
- Branching Out: A New Public Library Service (1998).

The latest **Social Partnership Agreement** (2006), *Towards 2016: Ten-Year Framework Social Partnership Agreement 2006-2015*, recognises the importance of recreation, sport and physical activity for the balanced and healthy development of children.

The National Recreation Policy is a continuation of the **National Play Policy** (2004), which was intended mainly for children of primary school age. The publication of the National Recreation Policy, to complement the National Play Policy already in place, will provide the frameworks to address the availability of amenities for younger children and youth-friendly and safe facilities for older children and young people.

The first two objectives of the **Irish Sports Council Statement of Strategy** (2003, p. 18) are:

- to influence the critical need for physical education in Ireland so that future generations understand the importance of physical activity and have the basic skills to participate;
- to increase opportunities in sport at local level and particularly for school-aged children in the sport of their choice at a level at which they feel comfortable.

One of the strategic aims of the **National Health Promotion Strategy** (2000) is 'to maintain health and support the development of healthy lifestyle choices for young people'.

Many of the recommendations of the **National Task Force on Obesity** (2005) are concerned with halting and reversing the prevalence of obesity, including creating the social and physical environment that makes it easier for children to be more active on a regular basis.

Reach Out: National Strategy for Action on Suicide Prevention (2005) identifies the importance of organised activities (sport in particular) in promoting positive mental health.

One of the objectives of **Partnership for the Arts** (2005) is looking at extending opportunities for children and young people to participate in, create and respond critically to the arts.

One of the goals of the **National Youth Work Development Plan** (2003) is 'to facilitate young people and adults to participate more fully in, and to gain optimum benefit from, youth work programmes and services'.

Branching Out (1998) identifies the Public Library Service as an important resource for children and young people.

chapter four

OBJECTIVE 1:

Give young people a voice in the design, implementation and monitoring of recreation policies and facilities

The case for involving young people

There has been a growing acceptance in recent years that children and young people should be more involved in decisions that affect them. The first goal of the National Children's Strategy is to give children and young people a voice in matters that affect them and to ensure that their views are given due weight in accordance with their age and maturity. This is in line with Article 12 of the UN Convention on the Rights of the Child, which was ratified by Ireland in 1992.

Participation can range from the provision of information to consultation and to involvement in the governance of an organisation. The participation of young people can be at national, local and organisational level.

It has been found that the main issues that young people want addressed in their areas include greater respect and decision-making at school, improved leisure facilities and transport, a more satisfying physical environment at school and in the community, and respect for young people in shops and public places (Borland et al, 2001).

For participation to be successful, it has to be meaningful to young people and for it to be seen that their involvement brings about meaningful change (Sinclair, 2004). Relatively little research has been carried out on the outcomes of participation. However, evidence from the UK, based on the examination of a number of case studies, suggests the following positive outcomes of participation (Kirby et al, 2003):

- **Practical benefits to services**
  Organisations in the UK adapted and developed their services to ensure that they better suited and benefited young people using them. This, in turn, facilitated better access and use of services, as well as higher participation rates. Changes often centred on physical site improvements, particularly play and leisure facilities. In some cases, new services were introduced by organisations to satisfy the expressed demands and needs of children and young people and to fill existing gaps. Examples included youth centres, information centres and leisure facilities such as skateboard parks (Kirby et al, 2003, p. 125). It would appear that young people have a more positive experience of services, are more engaged and feel greater 'ownership' when they were actively involved. Also, they use services more and services reflect their needs better.

- **Citizenship and social inclusion**
  Involving young people, particularly those who do not often have an opportunity to have a say, can lead to a deeper belief in their ability to change things and to a feeling of having a greater control over their own lives (Kirby et al, 2003, p. 134). Being involved in decision-making processes gives young people an understanding of political structures and, through this understanding, a motivation to take part in different forms of politics (ibid, p. 136).

One of the most significant outcomes of participation observed in the UK case studies was the development of positive relationships. Several projects perceived that relationships and perceptions of young people were more positive since their involvement in community issues (see Box 1).

> ## Box 1: Improved relationships with the community
>
> Following the regeneration of a park by young people and adults working together, a local resident made the following comment: '*See that wall? When it went up, I thought 'Uh-oh. But hey, haven't touched it because they own it.*'
>
> *Source*: Kirby *et al* (2003), p. 132
>
> ### Middlesborough Youth Inclusion Project (YIP)
>
> The regeneration of a local wasteland involved both young people and older residents in planning and developing the area. Middlesborough YIP brought these groups together to plan the development of the park. Before the environmental work started, the group put together an animated film about all the issues that young people and residents wanted to address. This has helped to change perceptions of young people and developed intergenerational relationships. As a staff member of the YIP stated: 'On arrival there was a big issue that young people were demonised in the area. They were blamed for all the ills in the community … We've broken that cycle in terms of lots of residents now really appreciate youngsters, and vice versa.'
>
> *Source*: Kirby *et al* (2003), p. 137

- **Personal development**
  Nearly all UK organisations cited personal development as an outcome for the young people involved in participatory activities. This included confidence and self-esteem, communications skills, group work and personal skills.

Young people's views

It is clear from delegates' reports from Dáil na nÓg that quality of life issues are very important to young people. 'Facilities for young people' has been a key theme running through discussions at Dáil na nÓg in recent years.

In the public consultation process for the development of the National Recreation Policy, there was a very high level of support for this objective (97% in favour). A number of respondents identified young people's involvement as one of the key issues in the development of successful recreation programmes for young people. One group of young people identified it as the '*key to all other objectives*'. There was also a strong feeling that '*young people should be listened to*' and that their involvement should not be tokenistic. Others felt that the involvement of young people in the development of recreational facilities and programmes, especially in their own area, '*needs to be a mandatory requirement in the development of any such facility*'.

The Government, through the Office of the Minister for Children (OMC), is committed to participation by young people and is actively committed to encouraging all Government departments, local authorities and other agencies to involve young people at the planning stage of policy proposals and new initiatives. In addition to being involved at the planning stages, young people should also be involved in the governance structures once the programme/project is up and running. Young people should also be involved in the monitoring and evaluation of recreation programmes.

Current position on participation

There is a strong emphasis in youth work on the active participation of young people, although it has been recognised that a significant reason why young people cease to participate in youth work (particularly as they get older) may be the absence of opportunities to participate in decision-making. This has been recognised in the National Youth Work Development Plan (Department of Education and Science, 2003a). One of the actions in this plan is that guidelines and criteria relating to the active participation of young people in all aspects of youth work provision should be developed, having regard to existing and innovative youth participation models (*ibid*, p. 19).

The research carried out in the context of developing this policy has shown that clubs that have a strong emphasis on participation by young people (in managing and operating the club in cooperation with adult leaders and in planning and carrying out activities designed to meet the needs of their members) do not show as steep a decline in membership over the teenage years as those who do not operate on this basis (De Róiste and Dinneen, 2005, p. 70).

The further implementation of the Youth Work Act 2001 also offers opportunities for the involvement of young people. It is intended that Voluntary Youth Councils will be established to advise on matters related to the National Youth Work Development Plan and to act as a forum for voluntary youth work organisations operating in the Vocational Education Committee area. It is envisaged that, where practicable, one-fifth of the members should be under the age of 25.

A number of programmes and projects with a recreation dimension do already involve young people in the design of services and in the ongoing running and evaluation of programmes once established. These include projects run by the Health Service Executive (HSE) and voluntary bodies, particularly those in the youth work sector (*see Box 2*). These projects, however, are the exception rather than the rule and young people's participation in the planning and development of recreation programmes and facilities remains underdeveloped. This is particularly true where there is not a specific youth focus to the facilities or programmes that are being put in place.

Box 2: Girls Active: A school-based programme to promote participation

Due to serious concerns regarding the physical activity levels of young people, particularly teenage girls, the North Western Health Board (HSE West) undertook a consultation study. Its aim was to identify the motivators and barriers to participation in physical activity by teenage girls and to obtain suggestions regarding the promotion of physical activity among this target group. As a result of the consultation, the following actions have been taken:

- The North Western Health Board, in collaboration with Donegal Sports Partnership and Sligo Sport and Recreation Partnership, works with 19 schools to promote the active involvement and decision-making of girls in programmes to promote participation in physical activities.
- Girls consult with other students on the choices of activities to be offered.
- Girls recruit the providers of programmes, such as yoga, dance and swimming.
- Girls promote the programme in their schools.
- Girls are active participants in reviewing the activities.

Source: North Western Health Board (2004)

An important structure for youth participation at local level is the local Comhairle na nÓg. There are 34 Comhairle na nÓg throughout the country, which are run by City and County Development Boards. The expectation was that Comhairle na nÓg would become a permanent and effective structure in local communities, ensuring meaningful participation by children and young people at local level and ultimately leading to representatives from Comhairle na nÓg being elected or nominated to Strategic Policy Committees and Community Forums, and having links to the local County Councils.

This expectation has been fulfilled in some cases: there are several excellent examples of where the local Comhairle na nÓg has been involved in local planning and development processes (*see Box 3*). But it is also the case that there is considerable variation in the running of Comhairle na nÓg, dictated in large part by the priorities, resources and circumstances of individual City and County Development Boards.

For this reason, the Office of the Minister for Children commissioned a review of the Comhairle na nÓg and Dáil na nÓg (NCO, 2005c). It is clear from this review that the Comhairle structure needs considerable development and investment in order to give young people a meaningful voice at local level.

While the Comhairle na nÓg structure is very important, there must also be meaningful involvement of young people in other local authority structures, including at a community and neighbourhood level. One way of achieving this would be through local Community Forums and Strategic Policy Committees, or the sub-committees of Strategic Policy Committees which could have a specific youth focus. This is already happening in one or two areas (*see Box 3*), but the process needs to be embedded in all City and County Development Board areas and must be properly supported if young people's involvement is to be meaningful.

Box 3: Dublin City Comhairle na nÓg Seminars

In 2003, the Dublin City Comhairle na nÓg seminars focused on the review of the Dublin City Development Plan 1999 and the preparation of a new Dublin City Development Plan 2005-2011. Over 500 young people — aged 7-17 from primary and secondary schools, youth groups, disability and minority ethnic groups — attended the six area seminars. The Comhairle seminars involved a series of workshops on particular themes. The young people used drama, artwork, crafts and discussions to formulate their ideas for the Dublin City Development Plan. The themes discussed were transportation, infrastructure, community development, open space and recreation.

Source: Dublin City Council (2004)

Apart from structures at local level, such as Comhairle na nÓg which provide young people with a forum for expressing their views on policy issues at local level, young people should also be consulted about the design of local recreation and leisure facilities, including public libraries, multi-purpose games areas, skateboard parks and community facilities. This has already been done successfully in a number of local authority areas. A condition of the grant scheme for the pilot project on skateboard parks, for example, is that young people will be involved in the design of the parks.

A recurring theme of the public consultation is access to recreational facilities. This is due to a variety of reasons, but may relate to opening times and to wider issues of the availability of facilities to young people. For this reason, young people need to become part of the local governance/management arrangements in place for facilities. There are a variety of ways in which this can be achieved, including having young people as members of boards/management committees, as observers on the board/management committee or as members of an advisory group linked to the board. This would be subject to any legal requirements that may be in place (e.g. membership may be confined to people over 18).

There is also a case for the local community to take the initiative to involve young people in community activities, such as residents' associations and estate management committees, which play an important role locally (*see Boxes 4 and 5*). Involving young people in community organisations, provided it is done in a meaningful way, will give them a greater say on quality of life issues that directly affect them (e.g. traffic management and local amenity issues) and will also encourage them to become more active participants in decisions and activities, such as estate management, affecting their own communities.

Box 4: Community participation — Kildare County Council developments

Kildare County Council's Estate Management/Community Participation Policy was adopted in 2004 to achieve the following objectives:

- to increase community participation within social housing estates and to maximise tenant involvement in estate development and community living;
- to involve other relevant agencies in projects;
- to involve youth in community development projects;
- to follow up on the tenants' seminar;
- to update the grants system for residents' groups;
- to continue with the Youth Endeavour Award and Tidy Estates Competition, and to build on their success.

Kildare County Council employs community workers to engage in selected local authority estates to encourage participation of all residents, particularly young people. Adults are encouraged to include young people by having representatives on the committees and the community workers facilitate this. This approach has been piloted in 10 estates. Indications are that it provides a sense of ownership and empowerment to the communities and counteracts social exclusion. Specific training and education courses were provided to complement youth clubs and mother and toddler groups run by the community, for the community. This holistic approach has been successful and has led to better relationships and a better quality of life for those living in the estates. Summer projects have catered for over 1,000 children and their families. These projects serve as a summer holiday for many who may not otherwise have this opportunity. The Tidy Estates Competition rewards the work of these groups. A Youth Endeavour Award has also been developed to encourage the youth of the areas to participate. Young people have participated in the Comhairle na nÓg, facilitated by the Community and Enterprise Directorate.

Source: Kildare County Council

Box 5: A Case Study — Bishopsland, Kildare Town

Bishopsland is a local authority housing estate about one mile from Kildare town centre. The area has been identified as disadvantaged, with many families feeling socially excluded and unemployment rates high. There are approximately 140 houses in the estate, which includes Fennor Lawns, Dunmurray View, Farrincooley Crescent and Ashfield. There are over 266 children and young people living in the estate.

A community worker started working on the ground in Bishopsland in 2000. The Bishopsland Awareness Committee was formed and supported by Kildare County Council. A community development approach was used, whereby people in the community were encouraged to get involved, identify their own needs and seek support to address those needs. Particular attention was given to the youth of the area by setting up a Youth Committee to carry out a needs analysis of the estate. The issues that were identified initially were more child- and youth-orientated facilities and activities. As a result of this, a vandal-proof community cabin was put into the estate to provide a play group for the purpose of community development. The activities (e.g. after-schools club, youth club) kept growing and developing, so much so that a local shop in the estate was given to the community as a temporary measure to house the growing activities.

From the start of this project, young people have been to the fore in the efforts of the local community and their participation has always been encouraged. A youth representative sits on the Awareness Committee and has been the recipient of the Youth Endeavour Award from Kildare County Council for the past two years. He was also nominated for the Presidential Award and has become an excellent role model for other young people in the estate.

Source: Kildare County Council

The Office of the Minister for Children, in conjunction with the Children's Rights Alliance and the National Youth Council of Ireland, published *Young Voices: Guidelines on how to involve children and young people in your work* in June 2005. These guidelines were for use by agencies and organisations in the statutory and non-statutory sectors to explore ways in which they can develop a culture of participation by children and young people. They show how participation can become an integral part of an organisation's policy-making, planning and activities, and provide practical guidance on initiating and developing different forms of involvement.

Actions to support the achievement of Objective 1

- A condition of funding for projects/programmes arising as a result of the National Recreation Policy will be that young people will be consulted and actively involved in the design, planning and, where appropriate, management of facilities and programmes. Young people will also be involved in the post-evaluation of recreation programmes.
- Consultations undertaken in relation to the provision of recreational facilities will include young people. This would include facilities where they are one of the user groups, as well as where the facility is designed specifically for them.
- Guidelines and criteria for the active participation of young people in all aspects of youth work provision (including governance) will be developed as recommended under the National Youth Work Development Plan. These will be phased in as part of the requirements for statutory funding of youth work organisations and initiatives.
- While recognising that the Youth Work Act 2001 provides for the inclusion of young people under the age of 25 on Voluntary Youth Councils, special efforts will be made to include young people under 18, where practicable, on the councils.
- The Office of the Minister for Children will advise public bodies and monitor the implementation of the participation guidelines, *Young Voices*.
- Arising from the review of the Comhairle na nÓg structure, the Comhairle na nÓg Implementation Group, established by the Office of the Minister for Children, will make recommendations to ensure the development of effective Comhairle na nÓg under each City and County Development Board.
- Local authorities will utilise the Comhairle na nÓg structure to inform relevant City and County Strategies/Plans, particularly in relation to recreational facilities and community and amenity programmes.
- Local authorities will encourage young people to participate on relevant sub-committees and through the Community and Voluntary Forums to avail of opportunities to become members of Strategic Policy Committees, particularly those addressing community, recreation and amenity issues.
- Local authorities will maximise the use of existing mechanisms to provide for young people's involvement in Estate Management Committees.

chapter five

OBJECTIVE 2:

Promote organised activities for young people and examine ways to motivate them to be involved

Following the public consultation on this policy, the text of Objective 2 was altered to promote organised activities rather than structured recreation. The term 'structured recreation' is a recognised term in the international literature and describes activities that young people choose to do and which include some element of being instructed and developing skills. However, it was clear from the public consultation that a number of people — teenagers in the 15-17 age group and adults alike — had difficulty with this term because they felt it implied too much adult control. As one participant said: '*I think there should be less focus on structured activities … I feel young people can create their own fun, they just need a space that is theirs to do so. When activities become too structured, they lose most of the excitement*' (OMC, 2006).

As against this, the public consultation also showed that when young people were asked to identify what worked well for them, they included many examples of what could be termed 'structured recreation', including youth clubs, sports clubs, drama, dance and music. With regard to youth clubs, those identified as working best seem to have a balance between having a structure and the teenagers themselves being active participants in the organisation of the club.

Structured recreation, such as participation in clubs, games, art, music and hobbies, has developmental benefits. Research indicates that participation in organised activities can enhance emotional adjustment, encourage pro-social behaviour and provide benefits associated with membership of a group. Participation also affects later educational and occupational achievement, and shapes adult leisure patterns (Verma and Larson, 2003). There are positive physical, psychological and social benefits to be derived from structured recreation. However, the acquisition of these benefits depends largely on participation in appropriate programmes and on the social environment in which the activity takes place (Laidlaw Foundation, 2001).

Irish teenagers are involved in a wide range of recreational activities, ranging from music, dance and art to involvement in sport and youth clubs. Significant findings emerging from the research carried out for this policy (De Róiste and Dinneen, 2005) include:
- Girls report more hobbies than boys. Boys report more sport. This is in keeping with findings from other research.
- Young people who are low in leisure motivation are less likely to report a hobby.
- Young people in the higher socio-economic groups report more hobbies. This may reflect greater disposable income, more free time and greater support/encouragement towards engaging in hobbies.
- Fewer hobbies are reported by older adolescents as compared with young adolescents. This reflects the move to more casual recreation through the teenage years.

Involvement in clubs

Nearly one-third of the sample (32.2%) surveyed in the research for this policy are members of clubs/ groups for which membership is required outside of sports/hobby groups (De Róiste and Dinneen, 2005). Girls are more involved in clubs than boys. By far the most popular clubs reported for both boys and girls are youth clubs/groups (68% boys and 52.6% girls). Other popular groups are the Scouts/Guides, choir/ folk groups and voluntary work. The popularity of voluntary and charity work may reflect the impact of the Transition Year Programme, which introduces many young people to voluntary work and to participation in organised events, such as the Young Social Innovators.

Participation in clubs and groups can enhance an individual's 'social capital' and their socio-economic development, social skills and relationships (McGee *et al*, 2006).

Participation in extracurricular activities, often linked to school, has been found to reduce school drop-out, particularly among those at risk of early school-leaving (Mahoney and Cairns, 1997).

Youth clubs/groups are among the most popular groups identified in the survey of young people undertaken for this policy (De Róiste and Dinneen, 2005). They clearly play a significant role in young people's lives, particularly in the younger teenage years. Youth clubs were identified by the majority of respondents to the public consultation as an example of recreation that worked particularly well. They did not identify a distinct preference for any one type of club. Some of the issues raised by young people were '*being able to relax and hang out with friends, and away from family, in a safe place*', '*having a choice over what to do*', there '*not being too many rules*' and '*liking the leader and others there*'. Many of the boys mentioned that they would '*like the club to have pool and snooker tables*'.

There are some 750,000 young people either involved or availing of services offered by youth organisations in Ireland (NYCI, 2003a). These aim to provide for the personal and social development of young people in a fun setting. The services are delivered in the main by national and regional voluntary youth organisations, such as Foróige, the National Youth Federation, Ógra Chorcaí and Catholic Youth Care and, in relation to the Special Projects for Disadvantaged Youth Scheme, by such organisations in close cooperation with the Vocational Education Committees.

There is already a comprehensive plan for the development of the youth work sector. The National Youth Work Development Plan 2003-2007, published by the Department of Education and Science (2003a), has four broad goals and recommends some 50 actions to achieve these. The plan is currently being implemented by the Department of Education and Science and the youth work sector on a phased basis.

Issues that need to be addressed

Several issues have emerged from the research that confirm what is already known by youth organisations and have been identified in the National Youth Work Development Plan. These are:

- **Drop-out**: 'Losing interest' is the cause of drop-out by older teenagers from certain youth clubs/groups. One of the reasons identified for this drop-out was that young people continue to be in a small minority in decision-making structures in youth organisations. Clubs where young people are involved in managing and operating the club, and where the activities are designed to meet the needs of members, are more likely to hold on to members as they get older (De Róiste and Dinneen, 2005, p. 71). The National Youth Work Development Plan has proposed specific actions on this issue, including the involvement of young people in all aspects of youth work provision, including governance (*see Chapter 4*).

- **Not liking the leader**: 'Not liking the leader' is a significant reason for young people to drop out of organised activities, including groups/clubs. This suggests the need for further training of volunteers and youth workers dealing with young people in these settings. Due recognition must be given to the fact that youth work has been as successful as it has been because of the goodwill and voluntary effort of community-spirited individuals (Department of Education and Science, 2003a) and that any move towards training and qualifications should continue to recognise and reward the commitment and qualities of such individuals.

- **Inadequate information**: 'Not knowing how to join' a youth club was identified as the most significant barrier. The general lack of information on recreational opportunities is an issue that has been identified by young people from Dáil na nÓg. This issue is one that needs to be addressed by all providers of recreational opportunities for young people (*for further discussion, see Chapter 10*).

Volunteering

The energy, commitment and enthusiasm of young people is a valuable resource that can be used for the benefit of the wider community, as well as for young people themselves. One of the ways of harnessing this energy and enthusiasm is through volunteering. This can be either young people volunteering in their community or volunteering to become leaders in clubs/groups of which they are members. A key objective of many youth organisations is to encourage young people to volunteer within those organisations and to contribute to the effective running of the organisation (*see Box 6*).

Box 6: No Name Clubs

At the start of every year, the No Name Clubs' committee seeks and selects a core group of young leaders from the older age groups in the schools and community to help them inform and run the clubs for a year. This is usually done through advertisement and interview. Once selected, all of the new recruits undergo a course in leadership and self-development. These young people are vital to the success of the clubs.

Further information: www.nonameclub.ie

Volunteering has many potential benefits, both for the young people themselves and for those they are helping. Young volunteers are likely to develop new skills and an increased sense of responsibility and understanding. They may mix with new people they might not normally encounter and strengthen links between generations within a community. Volunteering can empower young people and demonstrate to them and others that they can make a difference (Edwards and Hatch, 2003).

During the last decade, there have been efforts to promote volunteering among young people through the education system and national/local youth volunteering awards, as well as through the youth work sector.

Education sector

Evidence of voluntary activity is particularly strong in Transition Year, which has acted as a catalyst for the promotion of volunteering despite the absence of any explicit mention of volunteering in the Transition Year Guidelines. The fact that young people are free from the pressure of exams gives them the opportunity to engage in a wide range of activities, including voluntary work, in which they may not otherwise have the opportunity to participate. However, not all schools participate in the Transition Year. This is particularly true of schools in disadvantaged areas (Smyth *et al*, 2004). There is also the challenge of maintaining an involvement in voluntary activity beyond Transition Year.

National and local youth volunteering awards

Several of these awards have been established in recent years with the aim of promoting volunteering among young people.

- **Gaisce** (The President's Award) is open to all young people between the ages of 15-25. The award seeks to promote personal development by setting a challenge in four different areas, one of which is community involvement.
- **The Young Social Innovators Award** was established in 2001 with the intention of encouraging young people to get involved in social issues at both local and national level. The Young Social Innovators

Showcase involves Transition Year students in identifying social needs and in developing strategies to address them, in conjunction with local community and statutory organisations (*see Box 7*). The award is financially supported by the Department of Community, Rural and Gaeltacht Affairs, which has allocated €900,000 to the project for a 3-year period starting in 2005. Other Gold Partners and Friends of the Young Social Innovators are Irish Aid, Department of Social and Family Affairs, Combat Poverty Agency, Famine Commemoration Fund, Department of Education and Science, FETAC, Irish Youth Foundation, Trócaire and the Office of the Minister for Children.

- **The Young Citizen Award** was announced in October 2005 to mark the 2005 European Year of Citizenship through Education. The main purpose of this award, which was endorsed by the President and aimed at young people aged 12-25, was to formally recognise and acknowledge the voluntary commitment of young people as active citizens and to encourage them to continue this into their adult lives.
- Other organisations, such as the Lions Clubs, also sponsor awards aimed at young people.

Box 7: Young Social Innovators 2006

In 2006, over 3,400 young people from all over Ireland participated in 230 projects as part of the Young Social Innovators programme. That year saw the introduction of 'Speak Out' forums for students at seven locations around the country. Over 2,000 young people attended the forums, which provided them with the opportunity to speak out on the social issues that concern and affect them. At the Showcase in Dublin's City West, some 2,300 young people exhibited 144 projects.

Source: Young Social Innovators (2006)

Youth work sector

The youth work sector also encourages volunteering in the wider community. For example:

- **Foróige's Citizenship Programme** is an out-of-school education programme that aims to assist young people to develop the values and skills of good citizenship. The programme empowers young people, enhances their human development and enables them to realise that they do have the power to make a difference in the world in which they live. The Youth Citizenship Awards of 2005 were presented to:

  Boher Foróige Club, Co. Westmeath, who renovated the historic St. Brigid's Well after it had fallen into disrepair.

  Castletara Foróige Club, Co. Cavan, who produced and staged a drama about drugs awareness. This drama was also written by a club member.

  Kileevan Foróige Club, Co. Monaghan, who ran a summer camp for the area's younger children.

  LEAP Project, Co. Longford, who ran their own 'Youth Bank' so that they could help a number of needy clubs in the area.

  Loughglynn Foróige Club, Co. Roscommon, who raised over €3,500 for Crumlin Hospital for Sick Children through a range of creative methods.

  Monamolin Foróige Club, Co. Wexford, who researched, wrote and designed a publication on the culture and heritage of their local area.

  Moore Foróige Club, Co. Roscommon, who revamped the area outside the parish hall in which they meet. This included painting a mural, planting shrubs and greenery.

  Skibbereen Foróige Club, Co. Cork, who organised a charity variety show that celebrated the heritage and culture of the area.

Despite progress made in recent years in promoting voluntary activity among young people, there is a need for a more explicit strategy to encourage youth volunteering as part of more general initiatives on active citizenship. In its October 2002 report *Tipping the Balance*, the National Committee on Volunteering in Ireland has identified as important the capacity to develop volunteering opportunities that are (i) fun; (ii) allow a sense of control; (iii) fit in with the priorities and timescales of potential volunteers; and (iv) provide opportunities that will have a visible, measurable or concrete outcome. In addition, the report identified that increased quality and delivery is required with regard to:

- recruitment processes;
- young people's access to relevant information;
- opportunities for the development of skills and learning through volunteering;
- recognition of the value of young people's volunteering inputs.

The Minister for Children requested the National Children's Advisory Council in March 2006 to carry out an examination of volunteering and to advise on the measures necessary to actively encourage, support and promote voluntary activity among children and young people. The main aim of the research was to examine youth volunteering in Ireland by giving full voice to the experiences and ambitions of children and young people in volunteering and to identify key recommendations for both policy and practice. The resultant report, *Research on Youth Volunteering in Ireland*, contained a number of core recommendations to promote volunteering and, in particular, the development of a National Youth Volunteering Framework to drive forward, support and monitor the development of volunteering among children and young people (National Children's Advisory Council, 2006).

The report was forwarded to the Task Force on Active Citizenship by the Minister in October 2006 to assist it in concluding recommendations to Government on measures to foster and facilitate greater levels of active citizenship among young people and on the issues that affect them on a local and national level.

Adult volunteering

Adult volunteers have a crucial role to play in facilitating young people's participation in recreation, particularly in organised activities. A recent study on *School children and sport in Ireland* found that some 400,000 adults (15% of the adult population) were involved in volunteering for sport in some way (Fahey *et al*, 2005). Other sectors, such as the youth work sector, also rely to a great extent on adult volunteers. Despite them being a very important resource to children's sport and recreation, little is actually known of the motivation, capacity and needs of these adult volunteers.

In recent years, there has been concern at the decline in the number of adults involved in volunteering. The National Committee on Volunteering (2002), for example, stated that the rate of volunteering declined from 39% to 33% between 1992 and 1997/1998. In addition to the increasing pressure on people's time, there are also concerns that fears of litigation are contributing to the decline in adult volunteering.

The Task Force on Active Citizenship is to recommend measures that could be taken as part of public policy to facilitate and encourage more active citizenship in all aspects of life.

The arts and young people

The research carried out for this policy identified a very high level of interest and participation in the arts (De Róiste and Dinneen, 2005). This is particularly true of girls through their teenage years.

The UN Convention on the Rights of the Child recognises the right of children and young people to participate freely in cultural life and the arts. The National Youth Council of Ireland sees youth culture as being expressed in a variety of different media, ranging from popular music to digital photography, which by their very nature do not fit into a traditional view of the arts, but which reflect their interest in the arts in its broadest sense (*see Box 8*).

Box 8: View of National Youth Council of Ireland

'It is important that these activities are given due recognition as being legitimate and vital components of both our own and the wider global culture. This is particularly true in terms of the framework they provide for young people to explore their own identity and how they relate to the wider social and cultural world.'

Source: NYCI (2003a)

In the research conducted for this policy, there are many activities undertaken by young people that reflect their interest in the arts in this broader sense (De Róiste and Dinneen, 2005). Over four-fifths of the young people sampled reported listening to music every day or most days. This finding is in accordance with international research, which shows that listening to music ranks very highly as a free-time activity among adolescents (Child Accident Prevention Trust, 2002; Stiles *et al*, 1993). A shared taste in music is one of the more common shared features of adolescent friendship groups (Thurlow, 2002). It has also been argued that repeated exposure to music cultivates existing personal attributes, develops individualisation and may influence the person's level of self-awareness (Hansen and Hansen, 1990; Larson, 1995; Steel and Browne, 1995).

Listening to music during the teenage years is often related to developmental issues, such as autonomy, identity, love and sexuality (Larson, 1995; Larson and Kubey, 1983; Mainprize, 1985; Schwartz and Fouts, 1998). In addition to listening to music in their own home, there are a number of music activities that are very popular among teenagers, both as participants and as members of an audience — such as 'Battle of the Bands'.

Opportunities for physical activity are presented in many arts activities, such as dance, theatre and circus. This is particularly important in view of the drop-off in physical activity by girls during their teenage years. Dance emerged from the research as the most popular hobby for girls. The reasons for its popularity were linked to sociability ('*It's an enjoyable way to meet new friends*'), pleasure ('*It's fun, enjoyable, makes you feel good*'), escapism ('*Takes your mind off things*'), health and fitness ('*Keeps you fit*') and relaxation ('*It's relaxing*'). For girls from within the Traveller community, dance is a very popular activity engaged in through their youth club or simply with friends on an informal basis or in discos. Dance (mainly hip-hop and other popular dance forms) is also the most frequently quoted 'like to join' activity by girls, followed closely by drama.

The popularity of dance for adolescent girls has been identified in a number of international studies (Dowda *et al*, 2004; Hendry *et al*, 1993; Passmore and French, 2001). It has been proposed that dance contributes to an enhanced self-mastery: being in charge of the body can contribute to positive self-perception, body image and self-esteem (Hanna, 1988).

While there has been growth in recent years in the number of youth theatres around the country, due in large measure to the National Association of Youth Drama, other art forms such as dance have not developed to the same extent, with notable exceptions (*see Box 9*). It should also be recognised, however, that all forms of youth dance do not necessarily require formal structures. Teenage girls are interested in hip-hop and other forms of dance that can be provided relatively easily if a facility and a dance teacher are available.

Box 9: Limerick Youth Dance Company

Daghdha Dance Company in conjunction with Limerick Youth Services established the Limerick Youth Dance Company to meet the need for creative dance expression by young people in the city. The group, all female, aged 12-16, was primarily recruited through youth clubs and projects throughout the city and its suburbs. According to Daghdha's liaison officer: '*Dance is a great leveler. People of all ages and backgrounds have the ability to dance once they are nurtured and given the opportunity … we are now particularly encouraging boys or people who have been excluded from dance because of financial or other constraints.*'

Source: www.youth.ie/arts/in2

There is an increasing body of international evidence on the impact of participation in the arts, in an out-of-school context, on young people's growth and development (Cowling, 2004). The arts are also a very powerful way of combating racism and exploring cultural, ethnic and gender values (NYCI, 2003a).

Research shows that young people experience the arts in a variety of settings. In addition to the formal education system, they experience the arts through:
- arts within youth work;
- involvement in the services and provision of professional arts organisations;
- dedicated youth arts work with young people (youth drama, youth dance).

In addition to recognising the need to legitimise and support the informal, ad hoc nature of many young people's engagement in artistic practices, an Arts Council report (Coughlan, 2002) identified five structured avenues of participation (other than in a schools context) through which young people commonly access opportunities to participate in arts activities. These are:
- Dedicated youth arts organisations, e.g. youth theatres, youth orchestras, youth dance groups, young film-making, youth choirs.
- Youth and community organisations offering arts experiences for young people as part of a broader spectrum of youth or community work, e.g. voluntary, statutory and diocesan youth organisations.
- Arts organisations offering programmes that target young people as part of wider arts provision, e.g. outreach/education programmes, arts centres, local authority arts offices.
- Audience, e.g. as listeners, viewers, readers and consumers of arts products, including those that directly target young people as audiences.
- Formation of young artists, e.g. bursaries, mentoring schemes, apprenticeships, commissions, events designed to develop young talent.

There are many arts organisations specialising in specific programmes for young people. The National Association for Youth Drama, for example, advocates a way of 'working through drama… which emphasises personal and social development equally with the attainment of artistic excellence' (Cronin, 2001).

There is a close working relationship between the Arts Council, the Department of Education and Science, and the National Youth Council of Ireland (NYCI). The National Youth Arts Programme, operated through the NYCI, deals primarily with arts programmes in the youth services sector. The National Youth Arts Programme Strategic Plan 2003-2006, published by the NYCI (2003b), identified the following priorities:

- building strategic commitment to youth arts in relevant Government agencies and departments, and in arts and youth organisations;
- broadening the range of art forms being explored with young people and developing a range of mechanisms aimed at ensuring greater participation and quality youth arts experiences for young people;
- providing a range of support mechanisms addressing the information, education, training and networking needs of artists and youth workers.

While youth arts was traditionally seen as a recreational tool to achieve youth work goals, there has been a shift in attitude towards youth arts which recognises that all organisations, servicing both arts and youth, have their part to play in the creative development of young people. As Coughlan (2002) stated in his report to the Arts Council: 'It is the inherent value of the arts and the unique nature of art as part of human experience that is to the forefront … [young people] are entitled to quality arts experiences as citizens in their own right.'

The National Youth Council of Ireland sets out its policy on young people and the arts in its document *Arts in their lives* (NYCI, 2003a). The policy recognises that 'despite much growth having taken place, activity, in terms of youth organisations and services working in the arts, is still ad hoc and tends to be worker rather than policy-led'.

The Arts Council's document *Partnership for the Arts* sets out the framework of values, principles and goals that will guide the Arts Council in its work during the next five years (Arts Council, 2005). One of its stated objectives is to '*create better opportunities for young people to experience the arts*'. The action plan for the period 2006-2010 emphasises the need for children and young people to participate in and create and respond critically to the arts, and the need to recognise the authenticity of young people's forms of artistic expression, without which Ireland's cultural life would be poorer.

Cultural institutions

Research commissioned by the Gulbenkian Foundation and the Arts Council of England suggests that attendance at galleries and cultural events decreases during the adolescent years, so that the mid-teens are associated with particularly low levels of audience involvement. Physical and psychological barriers, gender and background were some of the factors identified that prevent young people from attending cultural venues. It was also argued that young people felt that cultural venues and what they have to offer do not appear to be relevant to them (Harland and Kinder, 1999).

In Ireland, the National Cultural Institutions is a group consisting of the Arts Council, Chester Beatty Library, Heritage Council, Irish Museum of Modern Art, National Archives of Ireland, National Concert Hall, National Gallery of Ireland, National Library of Ireland, National Museum of Ireland and National Theatre Society Ltd. These institutions are repositories and guardians of much of the accumulated cultural wealth of the country. They recognise that publicly funded cultural resources have a particular responsibility in respect of children and young people (in school, community and family settings). As part of their education and outreach programmes, they have devised a number of innovative access programmes for teenagers. While there has been a significant amount of work done on engaging with students in schools, there also needs to be an emphasis on engaging with students outside of the formal education sector. It is also recognised that relative to the situation in other countries, the role of the cultural institutions in Ireland as places of learning and leisure is still an untapped resource (Council of National Cultural Institutions, 2004).

Work done in Glasgow, which has the largest museum, education and outreach service in the UK, suggests that young people should be provided for as a core service within the museum and not as an add-on (O'Neill, 2005). Important elements for including young people in a meaningful way would include:

- providing high-quality modern displays and activities;
- consulting with young people about what interests them and how they want to learn about subjects that are new to them;
- introducing them to the world as it is;
- representing the culture and experience of young people, past and present, in displays and temporary exhibits;
- ensuring that core displays are designed for young people and their parents/carers, as well as for other audiences;
- challenging destructive attitudes and behaviours;
- reaching out to the most deprived and excluded, as well as providing mainstream services.

The Per Cent for Art Scheme

The Per Cent for Art Scheme applies to all Government departments with construction budgets. The scheme allows for 1% of any construction budget to be spent on commissioning art. Traditionally, this has resulted in large-scale sculptures or pieces of traditional art being set up at various locations throughout the country, most notably along new motorways. More recently, there have been innovative developments in the use of the moneys generated by this scheme to involve young people in arts projects in their local communities (*see Box 10*).

Box 10: Breaking Ground

In 2000, Ballymun Regeneration Ltd. commissioned a strategy for the implementation of the Per Cent for Art Scheme, known as 'Breaking Ground'. This works with professional artists in a community context. The commissioned projects cross many arts forms, including literature, dance, music, film, conceptual art, sculpture, painting, sound art and youth arts.

A number of the projects were specifically designed to engage with young people in Ballymun. They included '7 Days a Week', where the group identified issues and themes important to them and explored them through mime, movement, dance and gesture. This culminated in a performance in Axis. The work was a collaboration between the mime artist Rowan Tolley, the Roundabout Youth Theatre in Ballymun, Munch the Ballymun Samba School and the Ballymun Regional Youth Resource.

Further information: www.brl.ie/breakingground

The Per Cent for Art Scheme has the potential to be used in a creative way to enable young people to engage with the arts. This is particularly the case given the extent of investment in major public projects, including 'Transport 21' which is due to take place over the next decade. This may be facilitated by the increasing number of artists willing to work with young people in out-of-school settings, as evidenced by the huge demand by artists for training on the NUI Certificate Course in Youth Arts, organised by the National Youth Arts Programme.

Promoting physical activity

The National Recreation Policy is not a physical activity policy per se, but there are a number of issues emerging from both the consultation process and research, at both national and international level, that highlight issues in relation to youth and physical activity. These issues include declining rates of physical activity, especially among girls, and the environment needed to encourage a lifelong involvement in physical activity.

Rationale for promoting physical activity

There is compelling evidence for promoting physical activity among young people. The Department of Health and Children recommend that all young people under 18 years of age should take at least 30 minutes of physical activity every day to maintain good health. However, it is widely acknowledged that most teenagers are not meeting recommended allowances, either through physical education, school or community sport and physical activity. This is leading to increasing concerns in relation to obesity, cardiovascular disease and other health-related adult diseases. There is a growing concern about increasing rates of obesity among young people. The World Health Organization blames a reduction in physical activity, combined with the increased consumption of energy-dense, nutrient-poor foods with high levels of sugar and saturated fats, for the threefold increase in obesity across the world in recent years (WHO, 2003).

The successful establishment of physical activity behaviours in youth has three important health implications (Riddoch, 1998):
- promotion of healthy growth and development, and enhanced quality of life;
- prevention of disease and developing risk factors that may be precursors of chronic disease;
- potential maintenance of this pattern of behaviour throughout adulthood.

Physical activity among teenagers is also associated with good mental health and is directly related to higher levels of self-esteem as well as lower levels of perceived stress and anxiety (Calfas *et al*, 1994). Thus, the importance of continuing physical activity contributes to more than physical health — there are also associated benefits to mental health and social behaviour.

Participating in physical activity and sport is also fun. Young people will stay involved in sport and physical activity if their earlier experiences are positive, give them a sense of achievement and provide opportunities to learn new skills. Focusing on fun, individual needs and maximum participation will encourage young people to stay involved at a level at which they feel comfortable, thus reducing drop-out rates and encouraging lifelong involvement in physical activity.

In addition to the enjoyment of participating in sports, games, dance and drama, many young people are members of clubs that provide all the benefits of being members of a group with similar interests. Sporting organisations have good local structures and make an important contribution to fostering a sense of identity with and a commitment to the local community. However, many young people talk about 'dropping out' of the structured club setting as they get older, often resulting in a missed opportunity to continue with lifelong involvement in physical activity. It is important, therefore, to foster not only a sense of the health and well-being aspects of physical activity when younger, but also to develop a positive attitude towards physical activity so that young people choose to remain involved beyond adolescence.

Participation in sport and physical activity

Research commissioned for the development of this policy found that 88% of young people aged 12-18 play at least one sport either recreationally or competitively (De Róiste and Dinneen, 2005). Slightly more boys (91%) than girls (86%) play sport. The average frequency of participation in sport is also higher among boys, with boys participating most days while girls participate once a week. It was found that soccer, Gaelic football and hurling were the most popular sports for boys, with basketball, Gaelic football and swimming being the most popular for girls. Participation in sport declines for both sexes through adolescence; however, the decline is more marked among girls.

Physical activity, of course, involves many more pursuits than just sports. It also encompasses, for example, dance, drama, aerobics, and other more casual activities such as skateboarding and rollerblading.

Declining rates of physical activity

The declining rates of physical activity have been noted in a number of studies (Centre for Health Promotion Studies, 2003). The decline is particularly noticeable during the teenage years. The onset of the decline is usually identified as occurring between 13 and 15 years of age. By the late teenage years, substantial minorities have developed sedentary or low-activity lifestyles (Fahey et al, 2005).

The drop-off in physical activity with age continues throughout adult life, usually leading to high levels of inactivity in later years. Therefore, getting young people active is important not only for their immediate health, but also for their future health (ibid).

Reasons for drop-off in physical activity

The reasons for the drop-off in physical activity are complex, but they may include the lack of alternatives to traditional team sports, such as football and basketball, and the emphasis on competitive sports in school that have little carry-over into adult life (Fahey et al, 2004). School principals believe that the main obstacles to raising or maintaining participation levels in sports and PE among second-level students are pressures of time from schoolwork, especially at senior cycle, together with inadequate facilities (Fahey et al, 2005). However, young people do not necessarily see facilities as a barrier; they are more interested in being part of the action than the quality of the equipment.

Implications and good practice

Consulting with young people

In terms of tackling the problem of drop-off in physical activity among teenagers, Fahey et al (2005, p. 90) suggest 'rather than aim to achieve a generic increase in the amount of sport for young people, a more useful approach would be to identify specific types and categories of non-participation, understand the experiences, orientations and preferences of the young people found in those categories, and design responses accordingly'.

The importance of consultation cannot be overemphasised. By consulting with young people, we can establish the clear reasons why they wish to be physically active and tailor the activity to suit their needs, thus helping to reverse the declining rates of physical activity. When linked with Objective 1 of the National Recreation Policy (i.e. Give young people a voice in the design, implementation and monitoring of recreation policies and facilities), this approach can ensure that young people are fully engaged in the activity and have a sense of ownership of it, which is more likely to maintain a sense of belonging and motivation.

Unlocking the potential of the revised PE syllabus

Schools have the potential to stimulate an early interest in all forms of physical activity. The PE syllabus in secondary schools, revised in September 2003, now offers the opportunity to set the foundation for participation in non-traditional sports and lifelong involvement in physical activity. This is because the new syllabus adopts a holistic approach to young people's development and incorporates a wide range of disciplines and a more diverse set of activities into their sport and physical activity. However, experience on the ground indicates that there are variations in the implementation of the new syllabus.

The new syllabus recommends two hours of PE per week for each second-level student (Department of Education and Science, 2004). However, recent research has found that students are receiving less PE per week than is recommended: the average time found was 69 minutes of PE per student per week, just over half the recommended time (Fahey *et al*, 2005). It was also found that boys get slightly more PE than girls and that younger students get more than older students. However, extra-curricular sport also needs to be taken into account in forming a more complete picture of the amount of physical activity and sport available in schools.

It is also the case that a number of core activities recommended in the PE syllabus for second-level schools are not available on the PE timetable in many schools. For example, dance was not available in 80% of schools and swimming was not available in 76% of schools. The traditional team and field sports, such as basketball, Gaelic football, soccer and athletics, dominated the PE timetable, thus limiting the range of activities available to students (*ibid*). This has particular significance for teenage girls, who have identified alternatives to competitive team sports, such as dance and swimming, which are high on their list of preferred activities.

Teenage girls who took part in a consultation on being active and getting active, undertaken by the Health Promotion Department of the North Western Health Board (2004) and the Local Sports Partnership, outlined the importance of having more wide-ranging activities available (*see Box 11*). As one participant said: '*It would be better if everybody got a chance to try out different sports, even to see which ones they liked. If we could do modules in PE … do a sport for about three weeks and then change to another one, that way the lads wouldn't be deciding the activity all the time.*'

Box 11: Girls Active

The 'Girls Active' programme in the North-West Region is built on a partnership between the North Western Health Board (HSE West) and the Local Sports Partnerships in Donegal and Sligo. The aim of the programme is to increase the number of teenage girls involved in long-term regular physical activity through developing more supportive environments for their physical activity. The programme is aimed at girls from second year onwards who are not currently involved in physical activity or on a school team. It favours non-traditional and non-competitive activities. 'Girls Active' provides opportunities for girls to make decisions about the type of activity in which they participate in their schools and for them to take an active role in organising their own activities. The programme also supports schools in the development of extra-curricular activities that appeal to teenage girls through training for pupils and teachers, support for the provision of activities, development of links between schools, communities and clubs, and networking with other schools.

By consulting with young people and designing activities to suit their needs, the 'Girls Active' programme has been able to increase physical activity rates and develop a positive attitude towards sport and physical activity.

Source: North Western Health Board (2004)

Partnerships

There are currently 16 Sports Partnerships and 12 Physical Activity Coordinators in Health Promotion Units across the Health Service Executive. Local Sports Partnerships are being expanded on a phased basis throughout the country. These resources can be used to encourage, promote and support physical activity among young people.

Actions to support the achievement of Objective 2

Clubs/groups
- Further resources will be provided to progress implementation of the National Youth Work Development Plan 2003-2007 and the Youth Work Act 2001 on a phased and prioritised basis.

Volunteering
- Management authorities of second-level schools will be encouraged to include youth volunteering in their Transition Year programmes.
- The Task Force on Active Citizenship will advise on measures to promote voluntary activity among young people and on mechanisms for maintaining and increasing the numbers of adult volunteers.

Arts
- The Arts Council will promote a local partnership approach with local authorities, the youth work sector and other relevant agencies to further develop arts provision and opportunities for young people.
- Local authorities will examine the feasibility of using funding available to upgrade existing facilities to provide band practice rooms for young people. The Office of the Minister for Children will also raise with the Department of Community, Rural and Gaeltacht Affairs the feasibility of using Dormant Accounts funding for this purpose.
- Public authorities engaged in large-scale public infrastructural projects will be advised that a proportion of the Per Cent for Art Scheme should be allocated specifically to innovative projects involving young people.
- The Department of Arts, Sport and Tourism, in conjunction with the National Cultural Institutions, will undertake research on how best to improve young people's access to the cultural institutions.
- Local authorities, through Comhairle na nÓg, will involve young people in local authority arts and cultural provision.
- The Arts Council, through Local Arts Officers, will work with the Irish Sports Council through Local Sports Partnerships and VEC-funded Sports Committees to provide improved opportunities for youth dance.

Physical activity
- Local Sports Partnerships will develop programmes to increase participation in physical activity, promote lifelong involvement and address key issues such as gender bias.
- The Irish Sports Council will include in its Strategy on Lifelong Involvement a greater emphasis on recreational sport and non-traditional activities in order to promote physical activity.

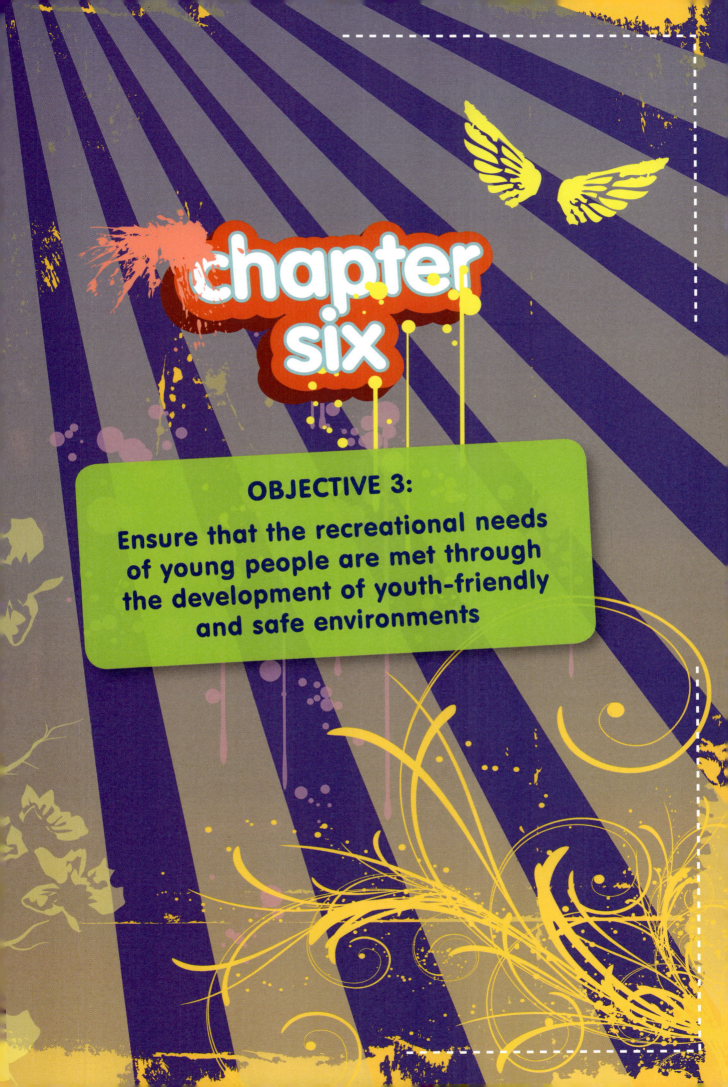

chapter six

OBJECTIVE 3:

Ensure that the recreational needs of young people are met through the development of youth-friendly and safe environments

While there is a strong focus on organised activities, particularly in the case of younger teenagers, there is also a move towards more casual activities that young people control themselves as they get older. These more casual activities can include skateboarding, biking and using the Internet, as well as just 'hanging out' with friends.

Friends are an important part of young people's lives. Talking to or hanging out with friends may fulfil important developmental functions for young people, including group membership and negotiating their own role within groups (Verma and Larson, 2003; Hendry *et al*, 1993; Connor, 2003; Van Vliet, 1983).

A longitudinal study on the leisure habits of 10,000 young people in Scotland, which commenced in 1987, found that activities, whether sporting or others, were a small fraction of what leisure means to young people. Most adolescent leisure is about 'not doing', about 'hanging around', about 'talking to friends', about 'being alone to think'.

Many respondents to the public consultation undertaken for this policy considered that such casual activity as 'hanging out' was an important objective and an essential part of the policy. The view of the National Children's Advisory Council was that young people's need to 'do nothing' sometimes is just as important as the 'doing or achieving' that often characterises their free time. Besides this issue, the following discussion also looks at the wider physical environment in which young people participate in recreation, as well as outdoor facilities for young people.

'Hanging out' with friends

In the research undertaken for this policy, over 90% of young people reported enjoying hanging out with their friends (De Róiste and Dinneen, 2005). Over half of the young people sampled reported hanging around outside 'every day' or 'most days'.

Locations identified for hanging around tended to be outdoor for boys and indoor for girls. Examples of outdoor locations mentioned in the focus groups included 'in the estate', 'behind the church', 'in the park', 'in the woods', 'at the [village] square', 'around the shops' and 'doing laps of the town'. Girls (only) added the additional venue of 'in pals' bedrooms'. Boys report hanging out in larger groups (10 or more) than girls, usually at weekends, whereas girls reported hanging around in smaller groups of 3-4. Older teenagers reported hanging around in mixed gender groups.

Hanging around outside can be problematic because it can be seen to be threatening to other members of the community and can result in more health-compromising activity for the young people themselves, e.g. the use of alcohol and drugs (De Róiste and Dinneen, 2005, p. 47). However, the normality of hanging out in teenagers' lives also has to be recognised. It is an important space for being with friends, chatting and doing nothing in an unsupervised adult-free space (Pavis and Cunningham-Burley, 1999). The vast majority of young people consulted in focus groups as part of the research for this policy enjoyed the fun and greater freedom they experienced in doing this, in contrast to structured activities or supervised spaces (De Róiste and Dinneen, 2005).

One of the main needs identified by young people in the public consultation was that they want somewhere to hang out with their friends that is safe, warm, indoors, affordable, relaxed, legitimate and where they have a sense of ownership. Safety is a major issue for young people and they perceive that there are insufficient places for them to hang out safely.

One participant in the public consultation summed it up by saying, '*Somewhere children and young people can go to play or hang out and feel safe without being afraid of getting kidnapped or abused*'.

Somewhere legitimate
Having somewhere to hang out that is legitimate in the eyes of their parents, their community and the Gardaí is very important. Young people realise that they can be perceived as a threat and that hanging out tends to have negative connotations. As one participant in the public consultation said, '*People think we look like ruffians if we hang around the main street*'.

Somewhere to keep out of trouble
Young people have repeatedly identified the lack of attractive alcohol- and drug-free venues where they can go at night as a serious gap in the recreational opportunities available to them. At Dáil na nÓg 2005, they also identified that hanging out in certain environments can lead to alcohol and drug misuse, as well as becoming involved in anti-social behaviour. As one participant in the public consultation noted, '*We need somewhere to go and hang out on the weekends and weeknights because we have nowhere to go and we only end up getting into trouble for causing harm*'.

The importance of attractive alcohol-free venues for young people was recognised in the Second Report of the Strategic Task Force on Alcohol (Department of Health and Children, 2004). This identified the need for alcohol-free venues for young people as part of a strategy for reducing alcohol misuse.

Somewhere to go during free time
Young people have also identified the need for somewhere to hang out in the evening, after school, during holidays and at the weekend because they believe that there are not many options available to them that do not involve alcohol or commercial leisure. One participant in the public consultation made the following points: '*There is no good focal or meeting point in my area where young people can simply hang out or socialise that isn't dominated by commercial interests … surely one doesn't need to purchase alcohol or spend great deals of money to have a good time. I find that there is simply no other alternative for people my age. I would appreciate the need for an alternative means for people to meet, make friends and have fun that doesn't have some sort of ulterior motive behind it. I think a good reason why this should be put in place is because it would save young people money and just have a space to call their own, away from the stresses of their studies and outside influences.*'

Youth cafés — International solution?

A number of international projects were examined in order to see what is being done to facilitate young people elsewhere getting together safely in groups. Several of these projects involve youth cafés.

In the UK, as part of a project funded by the Prince's Trust, 20 towns in the Scottish Highlands and Islands have established youth cafés, providing a safe place for young people to 'chill out' with their friends without feeling pressured into alcohol or drugs. As one participant in the project said, '*Youth cafés give a safe, secure place to talk with mates, play a game of pool, get on a computer or just watch telly*'. Plans to open more youth cafes in these rural areas are in progress (Prince's Trust, 2006).

In Australia, the police and Citizens Youth Clubs in South-East Queensland have undertaken a major change in direction — from the traditional emphasis on energetic physical activities, such as boxing and gymnastics, towards the provision of informal and unstructured space in 'The Pulse' youth cafés. These include state-of-the-art music recording and mixing facilities, as well as facilities for large discos and

participatory drama. Four of these multi-purpose youth activity centres were opened in 1998, three of them located near existing urban centres (Heywood and Crane, 1998, p. 35).

Youth cafés and drop-in centres in Ireland

In the public consultation for this policy, youth cafés and drop-in centres were frequently mentioned as examples of recreation projects for young people that worked well (OMC, 2006). The reasons given were that they are safe, well-run, cheap and a good place to meet other young people. As one participant in the public consultation noted: '*As a youth worker, I see the benefit that the development of youth cafés in the city and county are having in providing a space for young people to gather and interact in a safe environment. These facilities are also providing an opportunity to engage young people to put forward their needs.*'

There are a number of good practice models that can be used as a basis for the development of youth cafés. Some of these are supported by the Health Service Executive (HSE) in partnership with youth organisations (*see Box 12*). These projects have a strong health focus and offer a place for young people to access services and advice in a safe, non-stigmatising setting.

Box 12: The Gaf

The Gaf Health Advice Café is run by the HSE West, in partnership with Foróige and Galway Youth Federation. The Gaf has a drop-in service which provides a drug- and alcohol-free alternative to young people in Galway. By providing a safe entertainment venue with an emphasis on live performances, it maximises its potential as a drug- and alcohol-free entertainment venue. To complement the drop-in service, the Gaf has a work programme, designed by staff and the youth committee, offering a variety of information and educational services, incorporating a range of prevention and education strategies and offering health information.

Young people use the Gaf for a variety of reasons. It is a good place to meet friends. It is in the centre of the city in a quality space. It offers a range of entertainment (music, bands, acoustic nights and DJ nights) that is very popular with young people. Evidence suggests that talking to staff is one of the main reasons young people use the Gaf and a good relationship with staff is one of the main reasons for the success of the initiative. Another reason for its success is the involvement of young people in the operation of the café through a youth advisory committee.

Further information: the.gaf@mailn.hse.ie

The Gaf model combines a youth café/drop-in service/entertainment venue with an information/education service targeted at young people. As a model, it has the potential to be developed elsewhere. The following elements are essential to the successful implementation of this type of project:

- Young people must be involved in the planning process.
- A partnership approach (with statutory and other relevant agencies) should be adopted.
- The local community should be involved.
- In the case of larger towns in particular, the facility should be in a central location so that it does not become associated with one particular area.
- The building should be attractive to young people.
- Young people must be involved in decision-making processes at all levels so that they have a sense of ownership over the project.

- The facility should be drug- and alcohol-free.
- There should be a range of activities and developmental programmes offered for young people, as well as just a safe place to sit and talk to friends.
- The opening times should, in so far as possible, meet young people's requirements, e.g. it should be open in the evenings and at weekends.
- There should be a combination of salaried and volunteer staff.
- There should be a volunteer programme involving both young people and adults.
- Staffing structures and work patterns should reflect the requirement to provide a service outside of the normal 9-5 period.
- Insurance should be provided by the appropriate statutory agency.
- There should be a commitment to ongoing running or operational costs, as well as to the initial capital costs, by the sponsoring agency.
- The facility should be managed so as to ensure that it attracts a broad cross-section of young people and is not controlled by any one gang or group.

Youth cafés and drop-in centres can operate at different levels of service provision designed to meet the needs of particular areas. Apart from dedicated youth cafés/drop-in centres that require significant staffing and other resources, there is scope for using existing facilities to provide a dedicated space for young people to meet their friends. This may involve providing one or two rooms with sofas, vending machines, a snooker table and a TV in existing community/youth facilities, provided the environment is attractive to young people. Once a space has been made available to young people, it can be used to provide health and other information/education relevant to their needs.

In larger towns where there are established youth projects and services, youth cafés and drop-in centres can be incorporated into established services.

The larger public libraries have dedicated 'teen zones', with sofas, CD-listening posts, free Internet access, and multimedia and music collections. The availability of these services can draw young people into accessing literature, as well as information relevant to their needs. Public libraries have also undertaken innovative projects such as drama and drumming workshops, specifically directed at young people. Through the introduction of these new policies, 'the library' is increasingly seen as a place for teenagers to hang out. This is particularly true of new libraries in the larger urban centres.

Discos

'Discos are a safe place for young people to hang out and kept youth off the streets'
(quote from the public consultation)

Going to discos is a popular leisure-time activity. They were mentioned in the public consultation for this policy as an example of a recreational activity that works well (OMC, 2006). About one-quarter of young people attend discos on a weekly basis. Discos are often held though the auspices of youth clubs/groups, community or sporting organisations, schools and churches, as well as the No Name Clubs and Club for You (*see Box 13*). These discos meet a recognised need and provide an important alcohol-free venue for young people (De Róiste and Dinneen, 2005).

Box 13: The No Name Club

The No Name Club is a voluntary youth organisation, founded to provide an alternative to pub culture for the young people of Ireland. It regularly organises alcohol-free discos through its many clubs around the country. A club for young people, organised by young people, with the help and guidance of adult leaders, the No Name Club respects the individual's right to drink or not to drink, but it demonstrates and promotes a lifestyle where alcohol is unnecessary and helps to organise, influence and support young people in that regard.

Further information: www.nonameclub.ie

The research undertaken for this policy suggests that there are not enough discos for older teenagers, in the age group 15-18 (De Róiste and Dinneen, 2005). These young people do not have access to adult clubs and they feel that many of the discos that are available are designed for younger teenagers.

Discos can pose challenges for those involved in their organisation and management — challenges such as health and safety issues, or appropriate adult involvement. There are, however, a number of practical measures that can be taken to reduce these risks (*see Box 14*).

Box 14: Secrets of disco success

The Gaf Health Advice Café in Galway organised a disco for 450 young people on Junior Cert Results Night 2005. The organisers considered the following factors were instrumental in its success:

- The event was run in partnership with schools, the Gardaí, City Partnership and local youth services.
- Application forms were sent out through the schools.
- Forms had to be signed by parents and contact numbers provided.
- Parents were informed of policies and procedures prior to the event.
- Teenagers had to register on the night.
- Parents were informed if their teenager had alcohol on them on arrival at the venue.
- There was appropriate adult supervision at the event.

Further information: the.gaf@mailn.hse.ie

The wider physical environment

Youth-friendly and safe areas include dedicated spaces and facilities for young people. But the issue goes beyond this — to providing a youth-friendly and safe *environment*. Recreation occurs not only in organised settings, but also in the pathways around homes and schools, and around the buildings and spaces throughout the locality.

In a study of regeneration areas in the UK, it was found that young people placed a greater emphasis than adults on the importance of informal public space, as opposed to formal designated play areas (Elsey, 2004, p. 162). The UK Government's Green Spaces Task Force, in its study of parks and green spaces in England, found that run-down and neglected spaces had a detrimental effect on neighbourhoods (Department of

Transport, Local Government and the Regions, UK, 2002). This has implications for children and young people living in an impoverished urban setting, compared with children living in a more prosperous environment.

Outdoor places are considered to be very important for children and young people. If they are from families who are less well-off, the physical environment becomes more important, with the street offering an alternative to costly recreational and leisure opportunities (Matthews, 2001). This may be particularly true for young teenagers where street games can form an important part of their recreational opportunities (*see Box 15*).

Box 15: Community Games

The Community Games has introduced street games, such as hopscotch, rope jumping and tug of war, at its special activities weekends. The children participate in the area in which they live rather than where they go to school. This indicates that street games can be of importance not only in relation to their recreational benefits, but also in relation to local identity.

Further information: admin@communitygames.ie

Regeneration projects provide valuable opportunities to take account of the recreational needs of young people at the design stage (*see Box 16*). Providing expensive equipment alone will not solve problems around public space if young people are not engaged in the process of planning and development. Good practice would also suggest that in regeneration projects young people should contribute 'not only to youth-oriented projects, but to regeneration and community life generally' (Elsey, 2004, p. 162). This is particularly relevant in the context of the Government's commitment to roll out a programme of regeneration to all run-down estates nationwide, as stated in its policy on *Building Sustainable Communities* (Department of the Environment, Heritage and Local Government, 2005).

Box 16: Ballymun Regeneration

The Ballymun Regeneration has been designed specifically with the recreational needs of young people in mind. Before planning began on the regeneration of the area, a series of public consultation meetings and public participation workshops took place to find out what the people of Ballymun wanted.

The new development of Ballymun includes three large parks, with sports pitches, age-specific playgrounds and play areas, a kick-about area, gardens, a play orchard, a climbing/graffiti wall, pathways around the park for walking, jogging and cycling, granite seats at the main entrances, water features and a public square for local events, such as musical and theatrical performances. Other youth facilities that are part of the regeneration include a sport and leisure centre with a swimming pool, a Civic Centre, the Axis Arts Centre, five neighbourhood/youth facility centres and 'The Reco' youth centre. The latter includes the following facilities: a dance/activities hall, a youth gym for 15 people, a large Internet café, a computer training room, a Youth Information Centre, a youth café, a music room, a youth club room, a conference/training room with seating for up to 40 people, an arts room, a roof garden, staff offices and storage spaces for sports equipment.

'Hanging out' was also established as an important recreational activity for the young people of Ballymun during the public consultation. Therefore, the Ballymun Regeneration Masterplan aims to 'create interesting and if possible overlooked hanging-out areas, such as stepped banks or groups of informal sitting stones within housing areas and local parks and greens'.

Source: Ballymun Regeneration Ltd (1998)

Building sustainable communities

A new *Housing Policy Framework: Building Sustainable Communities* was approved by Government in 2005 (Department of the Environment, Heritage and Local Government, 2005). This sets out an agenda for an integrated package of housing policy initiatives. These include supporting higher densities and compact urban settlement through quality design in the creation of new homes, new urban spaces and new neighbourhoods.

The increase in residential densities has implications for the children and young people living in these new developments because they are increasingly reliant on communal rather than private space. Higher residential densities require that a much greater emphasis be placed on the quality (including the location) of communal open space and the ongoing maintenance of such space. High-density developments also need to make specific provision for the play and recreational needs of children and teenagers.

Planning Guidelines on Residential Density were published in 1999 by the Department of the Environment and Local Government. It is planned to review and update these based on experience to date with the existing guidelines and on changed demographics and settlement patterns. The new guidelines will reflect the need to build sustainable communities by linking the achievement of higher densities with a higher standard of residential environment, such as the provision of higher quality public and communal open spaces.

Following from the publication in 2004 of the National Play Policy, *Ready, Steady, Play!*, the Office of the Minister for Children is promoting the introduction of 'Home Zones', which aim to create streets shared equally by people and vehicles, and where the living environment and quality of life take precedence over ease of traffic movement (cars travel at 15mph or less). Home Zones, which are common in the Netherlands, Denmark, Sweden and Germany, help to foster a sense of community, improve safety (particularly for vulnerable users), encourage greater social activity and use of the street, improve the environmental quality of urban streets and create attractive places and neighbourhoods in which to live. They also encourage walking and cycling to local destinations and increase opportunities for children's play and recreation. A pilot project on Home Zones is being incorporated in the first phase of the Adamstown project (in the South County Dublin local authority area).

Public parks

Public parks and open spaces operated and maintained by local authorities are an important part of the environment to the extent that they provide facilities and amenities that are attractive to teenagers. Parks provide facilities such as tennis courts, football fields, basketball courts and pitch and putt courses, all of which can be used by the whole community, including young people. There has been considerable investment in playgrounds in recent years, following on from the 2004 National Play Policy. Playgrounds cater primarily for children aged 4-10, but they are frequently also used by older children in the absence of facilities more appropriate to their age. Multi-use games areas (MUGAs), with a range of equipment suitable for teenagers, are one way of addressing this issue. They are usually marked out for games such as soccer, basketball and hockey, and provide a central location where young people can gather and participate safely in physical activity.

Youth shelters

Partly in response to incidents involving young people in the UK, Thames Valley Police introduced 'youth shelters' as safe places for young people to get together. These are simple structures consisting of a roof and a seating area. They are open on all sides, enabling all-round visibility and 'natural policing'. They are developed in consultation with young people and with the local community. The most successful examples have been located near a sports facility, enabling a combination of physical and social activity. A number of demonstration projects in public parks, arising from the UK Government's Urban Green Spaces Task Force, include youth shelters (Department of Transport, Local Government and the Regions, UK, 2002).

Skateboarding

Young people often engage in more adventurous activities such as skateboarding. This takes place where hard landscaping permits, such as around schools, churches and shops, until it is stopped by the relevant authorities because of the perceived nuisance and/or danger factors involved, as well as concerns about insurance.

In Australia, the relevant authorities have taken the view that skateboarding has special requirements and particular potential for conflict with other users. Designated spaces are preferred for uses such as skateboarding, but they should still be visible to other users, both for their spectator value and for casual surveillance (Department of Urban Affairs and Planning, Australia, 1999). Meanwhile, in the UK, the Royal Society for the Prevention of Accidents acknowledges that skateboarding is a high-risk activity and that accidents will happen. The level and severity of accidents will be much lower if a dedicated facility is provided.

Ireland's Department of the Environment, Heritage and Local Government introduced a pilot scheme in 2005 to provide public funding to local authorities to provide skateboard facilities. Under this pilot scheme, 21 skateboard parks, in both urban and rural areas, have been accepted for funding.

Safety issues and safe environments

Safety is a big issue for young people, including safe travelling to and from recreational activities. In the research undertaken for this policy, about 15% of respondents said that they did not feel safe going to and from activities in the evening (De Róiste and Dinneen, 2005). The majority (two-thirds) of these were girls. Young people from Dublin are much more likely to feel unsafe than young people from any other county.

In 2002, the Health Behaviour in School-aged Children (HBSC) survey found that 86.5% of young people in Ireland reported that they feel safe (all or most of the time) in the area where they live. Despite this high percentage, Ireland ranks 10th in a group of 16 European countries, as shown in Table 1 (Health Promotion Research Centre, 2003).

Table 1: Percentage who report that they feel safe (all or most of the time) in the area where they live, by gender and country

	All	Boys	Girls
Belgium (Flemish)	92.0	92.3	91.8
Canada	94.9	94.7	95.0
Denmark	94.0	94.0	94.0
England	85.1	85.1	85.0
Estonia	85.6	85.6	85.7
Finland	97.1	97.7	96.4
Germany	88.5	90.7	86.3
Hungary	96.3	97.4	95.5
Ireland	**86.5**	**86.5**	**86.6**
Israel	43.5	44.9	42.3
Latvia	62.0	59.4	64.3
Macedonia	86.2	88.5	83.9
Norway	97.8	98.0	97.5
Scotland	86.4	85.8	87.1
Sweden	96.2	96.7	95.7
Wales	90.7	91.8	89.5

Source: Health Promotion Research Centre (2003)

Safety is not only an urban issue. It is also an issue for young people in rural areas. The public consultation for this policy found that young people in rural areas are afraid to walk in places where there are no footpaths and they are also concerned about speeding cars, particularly in the countryside (OMC, 2006).

Actions taken after the publication of the National Play Policy have improved this situation, with continued investment in the development of footpaths, cycleways and traffic-calming measures in line with Government commitments in relation to the national network of cycleways and the provision of new footpaths. But further action is needed in relation to this Objective 3 of the National Recreation Policy.

In the public consultation, the issue of safety was perceived to be very important in the development of youth-friendly facilities and environments for young people. Maintaining safety between groups of young people within facilities and environments, as well as between young people and other people in the surroundings of such amenities, were seen as important issues. It would also seem to be the case that in certain areas teenagers are very reluctant to move outside of their immediate neighbourhood and that this can result in them not moving from their own environment to avail of facilities if they perceive them to be outside of their 'territory'. This issue can be addressed by the introduction of appropriate outreach programmes to encourage young people to avail of programmes outside of their own neighbourhood.

Linked to the issue of safety is the adult perception of young people as a threat. In some cases, it has been difficult to persuade communities to accept new facilities, such as playgrounds, because they are concerned that they will attract teenagers in groups. It is possible that a number of the measures proposed under this policy will meet with resistance from local communities. This illustrates the need for the community to be fully convinced and involved when new facilities are being introduced. A number of steps can be taken to reassure communities about new facilities, such as the 'Planning for Real' method of consultation which involves displaying models of the proposed facilities as a mechanism for involving the local community (*see Box 17*). Other measures include installing CCTV and, in some cases, employing a Park Ranger.

Box 17: Planning for Real — Dublin City Council

The 'Planning for Real' method of consultation was used in Dublin's North East Inner City to gather young people's views on how a local park (The Diamond, on the corner of Seán McDermott Street and Gardiner Street) would be redeveloped. The park had become run down and was underutilised by the general public because of anti-social behaviour. The Central Area Office of Dublin City Council undertook a Planning for Real consultation to determine what the public would like to see happen with the park.

The Planning for Real exercise used 3D models of the location to be developed and a simple system of placing descriptive cards onto the model to allow people to air their views. The local school built the model and three information days were organised locally for the public to attend and give their opinions. Specific sessions for young people were organised through the schools in the area so that they could provide input to the consultation process.

The City Council had initially considered that the park was too small to retain the football pitch. However, this was a huge issue for the young people and after in-depth discussion they all voted to retain the pitch. A group, made up of a broad range of stakeholders including young people, drew up the recommendations from the consultation and, recognising the merits of the views of the young people involved, put the pitch at the top of the list of requirements for the new park.

Dublin City Council responded to the needs and requirements expressed and, today, the pitch consists of a 5-a-side football pitch and overlapping basketball courts. It is extremely well used and very popular with local teenagers and young people from ethnic minorities. The park would not have been such a success without the involvement and input of young people through the Planning for Real exercise.

Further information: Youth, Play and Sport Development, Dublin City Council

Research carried out on young people's relationships with the Gardaí suggests that there are a number of issues that need to be addressed to improve these relationships (Devlin, 2006). This issue (particularly 'hanging out' on the streets with friends) has also been discussed at Dáil na nÓg (NCO, 2005b). An important element of the Garda Síochána Act 2005 is the establishment of a Joint Policing Committee, set up between the Garda Commissioner and each local authority area. The purpose of these committees includes:

- keeping under review the levels and patterns of crime, disorder and anti-social behaviour (including the misuse of alcohol and drugs);
- examining the factors underlying and contributing to the levels of crime, disorder and anti-social behaviour in the area;
- advising the local authority and Garda Síochána on how they might best perform their functions in relation to improving safety and quality of life, while preventing crime, disorder and anti-social behaviour in the area.

Local policing forums may also be established within specific neighbourhoods to make recommendations and advise on the above. Since young people are an integral part of the local community and will be affected by many of the issues to be considered by the Joint Policing Committee and the local policing forums, there is a strong case for involving them in these meetings.

Actions to support the achievement of Objective 3

'Hanging out'

- Existing facilities should include a space dedicated to young people where they can meet their friends in a safe environment. A dedicated space should also be included as part of the design of new community facilities, including libraries, and facilities funded under the Young People's Facilities and Services Fund. Health and other relevant information, as well as education on a range of relevant topics, should be available to young people in these settings.
- Resources permitting and following a local needs assessment, dedicated youth cafés should be provided on a phased basis, particularly in areas where there are high concentrations of young people between the ages of 12-18. These youth cafés/drop-in centres should be introduced in consultation with young people.
- A formal partnership should be entered into with other relevant State agencies to provide health and other relevant services/information in these settings.
- An Chomhairle Leabharlanna, in association with the library authorities and the Office of the Minister for Children, will investigate ways in which to develop services in public libraries in partnership with young people.
- There should be appropriate community involvement, including the use of mechanisms such as 'Planning for Real', in the provision of outdoor facilities for young people.
- Joint Policing Committees will consider the participation of young people in local policing forums, when established.

The wider physical environment

- Young people will be active participants in regeneration projects, particularly in the design, use and care of public spaces.
- The Office of the Minister for Children will work with Dublin City Council and other relevant agencies to develop a youth-proofing model to facilitate local authorities in ensuring that young people are involved in their plans, policies and programmes.
- Adopting a 'Home Zone' approach will be examined in planning new developments.
- The Residential Density Guidelines, to be introduced by the Department of the Environment, Heritage and Local Government, will refer specifically to the need to identify at an early stage the preferred location of quality open spaces, as well as other recreational facilities, and provide for more casual spaces suitable for smaller children's play.
- Local authorities and RAPID will consider the provision of additional multi-use games areas.
- Joint Policing Committees, to be established under the Garda Síochána Act 2005, will examine the potential for the provision of youth shelters.
- Local authorities will review the operation of the pilot skateboard park scheme, introduced by the Department of the Environment, Heritage and Local Government, with a view to identifying potential opportunities for the provision of more facilities based on the recreational needs of young people in their areas.

chapter seven

OBJECTIVE 4:

Maximise the range of recreational opportunities available for young people who are marginalised, disadvantaged or who have a disability

One of the six guiding principles of the National Recreation Policy is that all young people should have equality of opportunity and access to publicly funded recreation (*see Chapter 3*). While this policy is aimed at all young people, within this group there are young people with additional needs who may need more targeted, resource-intensive intervention. They include:

- young people living in rural areas;
- young people from low-income families;
- young people who are at risk;
- young people from ethnic minority groups;
- young people from the Traveller community;
- young people who are ill;
- young people with disabilities.

One of the findings from the research carried out for this policy was the social exclusion from recreation and leisure activities and the discrimination experienced by certain categories of young people in minority groups (De Róiste and Dinneen, 2005). This was particularly true for early school-leavers and young Travellers. It is also the case that many of the barriers to participating in recreation identified for teenagers in general are compounded in the case of teenagers with additional needs.

In the public consultation for the policy, the general consensus was that access to recreation was a significant issue for these young people (OMC, 2006). There was also a strongly held belief among participants that young people with disabilities and young people suffering from disadvantage should be included in general recreational opportunities and should not be segregated from other young people while engaging in recreation. The Best Buddies Programme, which pairs a young person with disabilities with a peer without disabilities, was given as an example of positive integration through recreation.

'In my opinion, the Best Buddies Programme that is run in our school is one of the best recreational projects that I have seen. It works so well because the people who have the disability are treated as equals and not separated for their disabilities'
(quote from the public consultation).

Young people in rural areas

Young people in rural areas are disadvantaged by reference to their urban counterparts because of the difficulties they experience in accessing recreational facilities and programmes. Many towns and villages are too small to be eligible for funding to provide a range of services and young people must travel to larger urban centres to access facilities. Over two-thirds of teenagers in rural areas (68%), compared with less than half those in urban areas (45.5%), believed that there was very little leisure provision for them in their areas (De Róiste and Dinneen, 2005). This would exclude the major sporting organisations, such as the GAA which has a strong presence in rural Ireland. Swimming was one activity that young people identified as being particularly difficult to access due to the small number of public swimming pools serving rural locations.

Related to the lack of facilities, the absence of adequate transport to access recreational facilities and programmes is a much more significant issue for teenagers in rural areas than it is for young people in

urban areas. This is more likely to be the case with older teenagers and probably reflects the broadening of their recreational horizons (*ibid*).

The issues facing rural teenagers have been identified by a number of agencies. One of the actions of the National Youth Work Development Plan 2003-2007 is to provide additional support for youth work in geographical areas which research has shown to be underresourced in relative terms (Department of Education and Science, 2003a). This is important in view of the relatively higher number of rural teenagers who are members of youth clubs than their urban counterparts (OMC, 2006).

As indicated above, the lack of transport is a significant barrier to recreation for rural teenagers. This is a difficult issue to address due to the dispersed nature of the Irish rural population. The Rural Transport Initiative (RTI), established in 2002, funds the development of innovative, community-based public transport projects in a selected number of rural areas in order to address the issue of social exclusion. The RTI puts the onus on community organisations and community partnerships to develop local solutions to the particular transport needs of their rural areas. While young people are one of the priority groups identified under the RTI and a limited number of targeted services are provided to after-school and recreational facilities, the service to date has concentrated mainly on providing a much needed service to elderly and disabled people in rural areas.

The RTI is to be mainstreamed in 2007 in parallel with the implementation of Transport 21 and expenditure will be increased significantly. This mainstreaming provides an opportunity to examine ways of providing a targeted service for young people to attend recreational activities. Teenagers' needs in this regard are more likely to be at weekends: Friday nights, in particular, have been identified as a time when most need transport to attend activities.

Maximising the use of existing facilities is also important. This includes schools and existing community facilities (*see Chapter 9*). The Public Library Service, which operates under the aegis of the local authorities, is also an important provider of services locally, with 356 branches throughout the country and 31 mobile libraries. It is encouraging the concept of 'service' to its users being provided both inside and outside the library building (Chomhairle Leabharlanna, 2005b). It is also pioneering methods of delivering library services to remote areas through the increased use of new information technology (*see Box 18*).

Box 18: Taobh Tíre

Taobh Tíre is an action research project carried out by Donegal County Council with the support of An Chomhairle Leabharlanna under the Public Libraries Research Programme, with additional assistance from the Information Society Fund, Donegal County Council and the EU Peace 11 Cross Border Programme. The Taobh Tíre project is developing and implementing new and innovative ways to deliver the library services to remote and isolated communities across Co. Donegal, including two offshore islands. Phase 1 of the project includes the establishment of 10 new service points in a variety of locations. These are to be established in partnership with local communities and consist of a small collection of books, provided by Donegal County Library (a taster collection), and one or more PCs connected to the Internet, thereby providing access to the library's online catalogue. Taobh Tíre users can log on to the website and request items from any main library branch and have them delivered to the Taobh Tíre service point as soon as the item is available (Chomhairle Leabharlanna, 2005b).

Box 18 *(continued)*

Teenagers are the main focus of Taobh Tíre's efforts in East Donegal. A Taobh Tíre Programme is being drawn up in conjunction with the Resource Centre. Text messaging will be an important means of communication. Library staff gave introductory talks on Taobh Tíre and the library service generally to the local youth project. At the first of these introductory meetings, of the 29 young people in attendance, only one was a member of the library. Since then, all 28 others have joined up.

Source: Donegal County Council (2005)

As discussed in Chapter 6, teenagers are looking for safe places to hang out with their friends. The actions proposed in that chapter in relation to the adaptation of existing facilities to provide such venues is particularly relevant to young people in rural areas.

A pilot scheme for skateboard parks has been introduced by the Department of the Environment, Heritage and Local Government. This includes skateboard parks in a number of towns around the country. One of the pilot projects approved is a mobile skateboard park, which will be rotated between towns in Co. Laois. Such a facility has been established successfully in rural parts of Western Australia (*see Box 19*).

Box 19: Mobile skateparks — Shire of Gringin, Western Australia

The mobile skatepark facility has helped provide a safe place for children and young people to meet and participate in decision-making that affects their activities, as well as curbing feelings of boredom and isolation felt by many young people in a rural environment. The three rural towns of Gilderton, Gingin and Lancelin share this mobile equipment, designed to cater for all ages and skill levels. Through this initiative, the Council has solved the problem of providing amenities for youth in multiple locations and has won a National Award for Innovation in Local Government.

Source: Local Government Focus (2000)

Rural development and regional balance

At a strategic level, the National Spatial Strategy (NSS) for Ireland 2002-2020 aims to achieve a better balance of social, economic and physical development across the country, supported by better planning (Department of the Environment, Heritage and Local Government, 2002). The implementation of the NSS offers the opportunity to address quality of life issues. Providing improved social, amenity and cultural infrastructure will be particularly important to the development of successful gateways and hubs. In addition, the NSS also seeks to revitalise rural communities by enhanced accessibility linked with an integrated settlement policy.

The importance of the NSS, with its emphasis on achieving balanced regional development, has been underlined by the Government's decision to base the regional dimension of the new National Development Plan on the NSS. In addition, the development of the National Rural Development Programme 2007-2013 also presents the opportunity to address the recreational and leisure needs of young people in rural areas.

Young people from low-income families

The research undertaken for this policy shows that young people in higher socio-economic groups report more hobbies than young people from lower socio-economic groups (De Róiste and Dinneen, 2005). Similarly, in the study by Connor (2003) of young people in Waterford, the higher the young person's social grouping, the more likely they were 'to be physically active and in a greater variety of hobbies than an adolescent from a lower social class grouping'. It is also the case that young people whose parental occupation is professional or managerial are more likely to report familial encouragement than those whose parents are unskilled or on welfare.

There is a link between socio-economic group and the likelihood of money being a constraint to joining leisure activities. Only 13% of young people whose parental occupation is classified as professional or managerial identify lack of money as a constraint to joining new activities, while over one-fifth of those whose parents are on welfare or in unskilled employment report that they do not have the money to join new activities.

There is significant investment targeted at disadvantaged areas through local development programmes such as RAPID, which delivers a range of measures to disadvantaged urban and rural areas throughout the country determined by factors such as unemployment, income levels, family and social structure, educational disadvantage and high levels of rented local authority housing. Community facilities, including sports facilities and youth development, are among the areas prioritised for investment. RAPID is complemented by two further initiatives to help disadvantaged areas in provincial towns and rural areas — CLÁR Programme (Ceantair Laga Árd-Riachtanais) and the Young People's Facilities and Services Fund.

Other programmes also target disadvantaged areas, such as Measure C of the Local Development Social Inclusion Programme, provided by the Department of Community, Rural and Gaeltacht Affairs. It involves Partnerships and Community Partnerships developing activities targeted at young people who are considered to be educationally disadvantaged. It also seeks the involvement of key groups, such as parents, teachers and youth workers, to work with them in the programme.

In prioritising the needs of disadvantaged areas in the provision of sports facilities, the Sports Capital Programme contains specific measures to assist the development of projects and their likely impact on increasing sports participation, particularly in areas of disadvantage.

The Department of Education and Science funds the Special Projects for Disadvantaged Youth Scheme, which is implemented by youth organisations in cooperation with the Vocational Education Committees.

Despite these developments, recent research carried out with young people living in marginalised communities suggests that there is scope to improve existing facilities and amenities (Byrne et al, 2006). Such improvements could include:

- better utilisation of existing community centres located in neighbourhoods to provide drop-in centres;
- improved access to local community facilities from which young people may presently be excluded;
- improved information on what is available for young people in their area;
- increasing the number of outdoor playing areas, including football pitches.

Activities during the summer holidays

Because of the length of the school summer holidays, this time offers particular opportunities for children and young people to participate in leisure and recreation. There is now a wide range of summer camps run on a commercial basis.

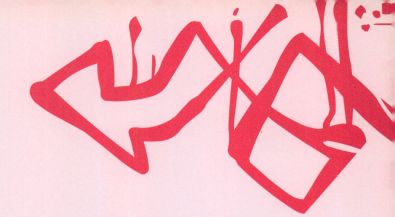

Local communities are actively involved in providing activities during the summer. Many run summer festivals, offering the opportunity to engage young people in carnivals, music, dance and street theatre. Specific activities, such as the Community Games, are run during the summer holiday period and provide opportunities to experience a range of sporting and cultural activities. There are also summer projects run by local communities, which are supported by local authorities though the payment of small grants. The involvement of parents in these projects can be an important first step in their subsequent participation as volunteers/leaders in the community. Thus, the relatively small investment incurred can result in long-term benefits not only to the children and young people involved, but also to the wider community.

At present, summer projects tend to be directed mainly at children and younger teenagers. There is a need for more innovative projects directed specifically at older teenagers, particularly in disadvantaged areas where the cost of commercial summer camps may be prohibitive. Recent research carried out on the free time and leisure needs of young people living in marginalised communities showed that once young people moved into mid-adolescence, they tended to move away from structured activities, including summer camps which they considered more suitable for younger children (Byrne *et al*, 2006). As one young participant in this research noted: '*It's for the younger kids really. They say you can go up until you're 16, but you wouldn't see many 16-year-olds going. If they were doing a trip to Clara Lara or somewhere like that, I might go. But other than that, I wouldn't bother.*'

There are a number of innovative summer projects directed at teenagers that, when evaluated, could be extended to other areas (*see Box 20*).

Box 20: Midnight Leagues

The Midnight Leagues, originally an American concept, were first introduced to Ireland (Ballymun) in 2004, targeting young people with diverse needs, aged 13 and older. The programme was delivered through Dublin City Council in conjunction with a local area management committee, BRISK. The programme combines sport and informal education. It comprises late-night activities designed to be both developmental and diversional, with education forming an integral part of the programme.

Midnight Leagues consist of a sporting activity combined with educational workshops. A sample programme might include a sporting activity and a 30-40 minute education session. Sample workshop sessions or topics could be drugs awareness, health promotion and anti-social behaviour.

Further information: www.brl.ie

Young people who are at risk

Groups that experience social exclusion are at significant risk for substance abuse, homelessness, crime and suicide, among other problems (Cleary and Prizeman, 1999; Connolly and Lester, 2000; Ní Laoire, 2001). One of the striking findings from the research undertaken for this policy was the extent to which early school-leavers (particularly boys) and young Travellers, who were the subject of focus groups, spoke of being barred from facilities (De Róiste and Dinneen, 2005). This included cinemas, pool halls, shops and other locations. The extent to which being barred was a consequence of inappropriate behaviour was unclear. Many of the young people interviewed report little participation in sports, hobbies or community/ charity groups. They appear to be barred from the few leisure activities that they do participate in and this

leaves them with little to do except hang around. The fact that these groups are already in educationally and economically disadvantaged circumstances gives particular cause for concern.

The consumption of alcohol combined with illicit drug use was a dominant feature of some young people's accounts of how they spend their free time (Byrne *et al*, 2006). This was particularly true of older teenagers (aged 15-18) and those not involved in structured or organised activities.

There is a small, but significant group of young people — 6% of those sampled by De Róiste and Dinneen (2005) — who are low in leisure motivation, i.e. they participate very little in sports, hobbies or groups. Many of the early school-leavers also fall into this category. This suggests that support mechanisms are needed to bolster positive leisure motivation in children and young people. Current research is looking at leisure education youth programmes as a means of empowering young people to use their free time constructively and to engage in meaningful leisure activity (De Róiste and Dinneen, 2005).

As outlined in Chapter 4, the active involvement of young people in programmes and projects (particularly community issues) gave them a deeper belief in their ability to change things and also a feeling of having greater control over their own lives. This was especially true of those who do not often have an opportunity to have a say. Active involvement can also lead to the development of positive relationships (*see Box 21*). Several projects show that relationships and perceptions of young people were more positive when they were involved in community issues.

Box 21: Community project

Over the past 5-6 years, the Community Development Section of Dublin City Council has been working with the 44th Whitehall Scouts in an effort to maintain a deteriorating scout den. However, by the end of 2004, the building had deteriorated to the point that the scout group could not get insurance for the building and there was a strong possibility that the group would be wound up. The estimated cost of the refurbishment was €60,000. The Scouts had less than €4,000. With the assistance of Community Staff, the Scouts were able to raise this amount, principally through the City Council (which subsequently raised its investment to over €120,000).

With the assistance of the Community Officer, they were able to recruit the Mountjoy Community Work Party to complete the required work. This work party consists of inmates from Mountjoy Prison, who, on being vetted and approved for inclusion in the scheme, go out each morning to work on projects such as this. The prisoners bring a wide range of skills and trades to the projects. The bulk of the work party is made up of younger first-time offenders, all of whom are drug-free. The projects selected all carry a high degree of community gain and ideally have a preventative function, such as providing safe recreation space for young people. The work is carried out to the highest standards and is supervised by staff from the prison.

On 15 January 2005, the Scouts and Cubs left a derelict building in the hands of the men from Mountjoy. At the end of June 2006, the Lord Mayor of Dublin and the Minister for Justice welcomed home 75 Scouts and Cubs to their newly refurbished den.

Source: Community Development Section, Dublin City Council

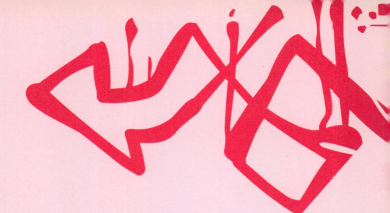

In the UK, the 'Positive Activities for Young People' programme provides a broad range of school holiday activities, including arts and school projects (Department of Education and Skills, UK, 2003). The objective is to divert young people from taking part in criminal activities and give those at risk of being socially excluded a better chance to fulfil their potential. The programme is designed to meet local needs, often in consultation with young people themselves. Funding is awarded through nine regional offices and is based on a formula that takes into account the needs of young people in a given area, local crime 'hot spots', truancy rates and community needs. The programme costs about Stg £25 million per annum and is funded by Government and the National Lottery. It has been assessed and appears to be effective.

In Ireland, there are a range of measures designed to support the personal and social development of young people generally and to provide targeted support to disadvantaged young people who are at risk of early school-leaving or of drifting into drug abuse, vandalism, crime and other anti-social behaviour. These measures include:

- **Garda Juvenile Diversion Programme** consists of community-based, multi-agency crime prevention projects that seek to divert young people from becoming involved (or further involved) in anti-social and/or criminal behaviour by providing suitable activities to facilitate personal development, promote civic responsibility and improve prospects of employability. The projects are funded by the Department of Justice, Equality and Law Reform, and administered by the Community Relations Section of An Garda Síochána. Areas and individuals are selected for these projects according to internationally recognised risk factors for offending, which include reference to socio-economic status and educational attainment.

- **Special Projects for Disadvantaged Youth** provides special out-of-school projects for disadvantaged young people, in particular young homeless people, substance-abusers and young people who are members of the Traveller community. The projects facilitate the personal and social development of participants, equip them with the knowledge, skills and attitudes necessary for their integration into society and enable them to reach their potential.

- **Young People's Facilities and Services Fund** (YPFSF) was established in 1998 as part of the Government's National Drug Strategy. Its target group is young people between the ages of 10 and 21 who are defined as 'at risk' due to factors such as family circumstances, educational disadvantage or involvement in crime or substance misuse. One of the objectives of the YPFSF is to assist in the development of youth facilities, including sport and recreational facilities, and services in areas where a significant drug problem exists or has the potential to develop, and to attract young people into these facilities and activities and divert them away from the dangers of substance abuse. Funding is also provided for Sports Development Officers, who use sport as a tool to redirect young people in disadvantaged areas into active recreation/leisure pursuits and facilities at a level that suits their needs.

- **Youth Information Centres Programme** aims to provide a network of centres giving information and support to young people so as to promote their personal autonomy and resourcefulness, enable them to overcome their problems more effectively and encourage their active participation in society.

- **Youth Service Grant Scheme** provides annual grants to support national and major regional voluntary youth work organisations with distinctive philosophies and programmes aimed at the personal, social, recreational, cultural and spiritual development of young people.

Community-based local initiatives of the Local Development Social Inclusion Programme are aimed at enhancing the social and personal development of young people who have left school early or who are at risk of leaving school early. Many of the actions seek to increase the range of community-based education and youth development opportunities available from early years through to adulthood.

The Crime Council has noted that young people who are in the greatest need of support, advice and recreational outlets are often the hardest to engage and the most difficult to work with (Crime Council, 2003). The Council has highlighted a number of shortcomings in service provision for young people, including:

- the lack of affordable and/or accessible facilities for young people in local communities;
- the need for more intensive street-level outreach work with 'at risk' young people, as a precursor to engagement in wider youth services and activities;
- the difficulties in employing staff to work the unsocial hours required.

Research suggests that if young people at risk are to benefit from the positive effects deriving from certain types of activity, they must include a cognitive and social component (Laidlaw Foundation, 2001). The young people concerned must form constructive alliances with their peers and instructors, and with the service providers associated with the activity in question. Activities that have these components should also be suited to the needs or be of interest to the young people in question (Stone *et al*, 1998). In that regard, one of the findings from the latter research is the extent to which boxing is a popular 'like to join' activity for teenage boys. The findings indicate that more boys would like to join boxing than are involved in the sport, but that there are certain barriers to joining, the most significant of which is the absence of facilities in their localities.

Young people from ethnic minority groups

Ireland is becoming an increasingly multicultural society. Recreation is an important way for young people from different cultural backgrounds to engage in activities together and to develop social networks and increase understanding. Facilitating contact between young people from different cultures can help to challenge racist attitudes and enable young people to get to know each other as individuals rather than as members of a particular ethnic group.

Young people themselves have identified the integration of people from ethnic minority groups as an issue. A number of the projects in the 2006 Young Social Innovators sought to address this issue, particularly in relation to asylum-seekers, and identified recreation as a means of facilitating integration (*see Box 22*).

Box 22: Living in a Bubble — The Life of an Asylum-Seeker

Alerted to the plight of asylum-seekers by an article in the local newspaper, a group of young students from the St. Louis Community School in Kiltimagh, Co. Mayo, set about this social issue on their own doorstep. Working with local support groups, the team made contact with asylum-seekers and found out that many of them felt isolated. The key word for the project then became 'integration'. The team set up a homework club and leisure activities for children, organised a float for St. Patrick's Day and ran craft projects in an effort to combat the isolation felt by asylum-seekers in the area and to promote integration with the local community.

Helping Global Children

The aim of this project, undertaken by students of the Mercy College in Sligo, was to create a different attitude to asylum-seekers within the local community. The students concentrated on a residential facility for asylum-seekers in their town. After their initial introduction to the parents and children residing at the house, they issued them with questionnaires. They made links with the local branch of the St. Vincent de Paul Society and contacted an Irish MEP regarding funds. As a result, they have provided recreational facilities for the children. They now dedicate two hours per week to these children, helping them with homework and taking part in art and sports activities.

Source: Young Social Innovators (2006)

There may be particular barriers to integrating young people from ethnic minorities into existing recreational programmes, including youth work services. These would include such factors as a lack of information, language barriers, differing levels of maturity, differing cultural understandings of 'youth', an absence of family support and financial barriers. There may also be structural and attitudinal barriers that need to be overcome in those providing the service (McCrea, 2003).

The development of an intercultural strategy for the youth work sector is included in the National Action Plan against Racism (NAPR), published by the Department of Justice, Equality and Law Reform (2005a). Work is currently underway on the development of the NAPR, which will be led by the National Youth Council of Ireland and the Department of Education and Science.

The sports governing bodies are showing an awareness of the need to integrate young people from ethnic minorities through the medium of sport. The Football Association of Ireland (FAI), for example, is appointing a coordinator to ensure, among other things, that ethnic minorities are provided with equal opportunities to participate in existing football initiatives.

Anecdotal evidence suggests that facilities such as multi-use games areas, which include basketball courts as well as other more traditional sports such as soccer, may be attractive to young people from ethnic minorities.

A Libraries and Cultural Diversity Project is being operated by a number of public libraries, including Meath County Council Library Service, Waterford City Libraries and An Chomhairle Leabharlanna (2005a). This project aims to explore how Irish libraries can provide a better service to the increasingly multicultural nature of Irish society.

Young people from the Traveller community

According to the 2002 Census, there are approximately 24,000 Travellers living in Ireland (CSO, 2004b). Of these, 10,000 (42%) are aged 14 or younger and just under 5,000 are aged 15-24. Figures for 2004 showed that there were almost 7,000 Traveller families in the State. Almost 75% resided in accommodation provided by or with the assistance of local authorities. A further 15% lived on unauthorised (roadside) sites.

Research undertaken for this policy included focus groups with a small number of teenagers from the Traveller community (De Róiste and Dinneen, 2005). The three main barriers to recreation that emerged from the research were social exclusion (being barred), discrimination and cultural traditions.

Being barred emerged as a particular problem for young men from the Traveller community. There was also evidence that they suffered discrimination from some sports clubs, which appeared to operate an unofficial quota system. On the other hand, other clubs welcome Travellers and promote integration (see Box 23). It also appeared to be the case that young Travellers had to hide their identity to gain access to facilities. As one young Traveller commented: 'Sometimes you hide your identity until you get in and then after a while you let them know you're a Traveller.' Another young man noted: 'When one Traveller messes, they put all Travellers out … imagine if they did that to settled people.'

Cultural traditions appear to be a significant barrier to recreation for teenage girls. At a relatively young age, girls appear to be discouraged from participating in sports and hobbies, and are expected to help out at home by cooking, cleaning and babysitting. Certain sports, such as cycling and mixed-sex sports, are discouraged. Young Traveller girls reported that this could cause problems at school: '*You're supposed to go swimming; they wouldn't take the boys as an excuse and even if you don't go you still have to pay for it.*'

The Report of the Task Force on the Travelling Community, published in 1995, recognised that participation by Travellers in sport and recreation activities is another way in which mutual understanding and respect can be developed between Travellers and the settled community (Department of Justice, 1995). The Task Force recommended, in relation to all forms of recreational activity and access to venues in which these activities take place, that discriminatory practices of a direct and indirect nature should be prohibited. This matter has been addressed in legislation through the Equal Status Acts, 2000 and 2004. However, it is clear that much remains to be done to counter prejudice and discriminatory attitudes. The National Action Plan against Racism, launched in January 2005, provides the strategic direction to develop a more inclusive intercultural society in Ireland.

An approach to service provision and related supports based on interagency cooperation has been approved by Government following the report of the High Level Group on Travellers Issues (Department of Justice, Equality and Law Reform, 2006). Interagency groups are being established by City and County Development Boards to develop a strategic plan for Travellers. While these groups will focus initially on such services as local authority accommodation, health, education and training, they could also provide a forum to help support a wider range of initiatives, including the recreational needs of young Travellers at local level (*see Box 24*).

Box 24: Travellers Youth Service

The Travellers Youth Service, which is funded by the Department of Education and Science (Youth Affairs Section), is the main provider of youth services to the Traveller community in the greater Dublin Area. Through social and personal education, Travellers Youth Service aims to ensure that young Travellers are able to participate in youth activities and by so doing, enhance their personal and community development skills, enabling them to take greater control of their own lives. The service is targeted at the 10-25 age group, both male and female. Currently, Traveller Youth Service works with over 300 young people in its catchment area, providing a mixture of recreational and developmental programmes. Outreach services are the main focus of the youth programme and involve working off-site and bringing the young people to activities not usually participated in. This programme includes youth arts, outdoor pursuits, cinema, theatre and museum trips, swimming and various sports. On-site programmes, including music, dance, drama and drug awareness, take place where facilities are available or in local facilities.

Further information: www.exchangehouse.ie/youthservice.htm

Young people who are ill

Hospitalisation can be a time of great emotional trauma, particularly for children and teenagers. Chronically ill teenagers who are in hospital over long periods can be isolated from their friends and normal support systems. The most common disadvantages of hospitalisation cited by children and young people were losing contact with their friends and siblings, missing home comforts and school, and losing freedom and privacy (Coyne *et al*, 2006). The number of seriously ill teenage patients is increasing; many more children with chronic and life-threatening illnesses, such as cystic fibrosis and heart disease, are surviving into adulthood and beyond. Consequently, it is important that their experience in the hospital setting is as close to normal life as possible.

Recreation in institutional settings is recognised as being particularly helpful in the rehabilitation and recovery process. As well as being an important component of treatment, it also enhances the general sense of well-being (Pedlar, 1995).

The types of facilities that young people are looking for are not particularly elaborate. They can be:
- a distinct sitting room or games room for teenagers;
- the provision of playstations;
- videos and DVDs that are age-appropriate;
- CDs, radios, books and magazines;
- a Play Therapist to assist those who are finding the hospital environment particularly difficult to cope with;
- recreational facilities in out-patients as well as in wards.

Article 7 of the Charter for Children in Hospitals (Alderson, 1993) was adopted by the European Association for Children in Hospital in 1998 to ensure that '*children shall have full opportunity for play, recreation and education suited to their age and condition, and shall be in an environment designed, furnished, staffed and equipped to meet their needs*'. This Article stresses the need for:
- An environment that meets the needs of children of all ages and situations.
- Extensive possibilities for play, recreation and education, which should be:
  - available in the form of appropriate play materials;
  - ensure adequate periods of time for play seven days a week;
  - provide for the abilities of all age groups cared for in the facility;
  - inspire creative activities by all children;
  - allow for the continuation of the level of education already reached.
- Sufficient suitably qualified staff should be available to meet the needs of children for play, recreation and education.
- The architecture and interior design of such an environment must incorporate appropriate features for all age groups and types of illnesses treated in the facility.

Trained hospital Play Specialists can guide and promote interactions with peers who are going through the same or similar experiences. In the absence of sufficient Play Specialists, much of this work is carried out on a voluntary basis by, for example, Play Well Volunteers from Children in Hospital Ireland (*see Box 25*).

There is a need for dedicated spaces for teenagers within hospital settings and rehabilitation facilities so that they can participate in therapeutic recreation and relax with other teenagers without interfering with younger or older patients (*see Box 26*). The lack of appropriate space is compounded by the fact that older teenagers in particular may not be cared for in paediatric wards or units, and that the cut-off point for their care in these units can vary between hospitals (in non-paediatric hospitals, where children are admitted, the cut-off age is between 14-16 years).

Box 25: Laughter is the best medicine — Young Social Innovators '06

Raising awareness of the benefits of laughter as medicine was the aim of this project in the Young Social Innovators '06 Showcase (Project No. 76). Students of the Loreto Secondary School, Balbriggan, Co. Dublin, made links with two hospitals for sick children, an airline company and a 'clown doctor'. They entertained sick children on board a flight to Lapland, as well as engaging in fund-raising activities, the proceeds of which were using to produce a fun CD. As a result of this project, the students have been invited to the next launch of Clown Doctors Ireland.

Source: Young Social Innovators (2006)

Box 26: Barretstown

Therapeutic recreation is the key component of the programme at Barretstown, which caters for seriously ill children and young people. The children who come to Barretstown have, to a greater or lesser degree, experienced a loss of control in their lives through being diagnosed with a serious illness. In Barretstown, children and young people are encouraged to take control of things that affect them and overcome challenges, whether it be leaving the confines of a wheelchair and climbing a tree, or singing, dancing or acting in front of a supportive audience.

The programmes employ the medium of recreation as a means of providing a range of specific therapeutic benefits to those served. The programmes are informed by a number of theoretical frameworks and disciplines, including recreational therapy, adventure-based counselling, occupational therapy, psychology and education.

In Barretstown, the environment is made therapeutic in a number of ways:

- A physically and emotionally safe environment is guaranteed.
- Physical limitations and obstacles to participation are removed wherever possible, with all activities adapted to the particular needs of the child.
- Close 1:2 supervision enables highly personalised support throughout the programme.
- All activities involve challenge. Participants are encouraged to reach beyond their personal 'comfort zone' into unfamiliar, often uncomfortable new territory.
- All challenges are, through careful guidance, met with success.
- Recreational experiences are processed, i.e. children and young people are encouraged to discuss and reflect on the experience and to compare reactions, with the goal of generalising and applying the experience to their lives in a relevant way.
- A balance of individual and group activities is provided, enabling personal achievement while encouraging trust and cooperation.
- 'Challenge by Choice' is an inherent component of the programmes, with children and young people choosing the degree and type of participation in activities.
- Interacting with children with a wide range of diagnoses and backgrounds reduces the sense of isolation and enhances empathy and tolerance.

Further information: www.barretstown.org

The development of a new national Children's Hospital, providing tertiary services for the whole country and secondary services for the greater Dublin area and surrounding counties, offers the opportunity to address these issues and make provision for the play and recreation needs of children and teenagers. The question of applying a standard cut-off age for paediatric patients will be a matter to be addressed in the context of the development of the new Children's Hospital.

Young people with disabilities

A total of 7,039 children under 18 years of age were registered on the National Physical and Sensory Disability Database in 2005 (OMC, 2007). The figures relating to intellectual disability show 7,385 children under 18 years registered on the National Intellectual Disability Database in 2005.

The additional needs of young people with disabilities are recognised in the National Children's Strategy, which states that '*children with a disability will be entitled to the services they need to achieve their full potential*' (Department of Health and Children, 2000a, p. 68).

Article 23 of the UN Convention on the Rights of the Child focuses specifically on children with a mental or physical disability. It promotes their right to '*enjoy a full and decent life, in conditions which ensure dignity, promote self-reliance and facilitate the child's active participation in the community*'. To that end, Article 23 asserts the right of children with disabilities to special care, to appropriate education and training, and to access to recreation opportunities '*in a manner conducive to the child's achieving the fullest possible social integration and individual development, including his or her cultural and spiritual development*'.

The benefits of participation in recreation for people with disabilities are considerable. People with learning difficulties appear to gain significant mental, social, spiritual and physical benefits from sport and leisure activities (Chawla, 1994). A study of the impact of participating in the Special Olympics shows that participation leads to a general sense of self-worth and improvement in self-esteem in athletes (Weiss *et al*, 2003).

Barriers and incentives to participation in recreation exist for all people. But people with disabilities often have to endure all sorts of additional barriers, including insufficient information and expertise on the part of service providers; family and peers; transport difficulties; lack of companions/volunteers; negative attitudes; lack of time and costs; poor PE provision in schools; negative school experiences; low expectations from teachers, family and peers; poor facilities; lack of coverage of sports in the media; and lack of experience of the benefits of physical activity (NDA, 2005).

Research undertaken for the development of this policy found that the main barriers to participation in recreation for young people with disabilities are structural (De Róiste and Dinneen, 2005). They include lack of transport, cost, inadequate equipment, poor access and a lack of provision and programming. Other barriers involve parental over-protectiveness and widely dispersed friendship groups due to attending boarding schools or travelling a long distance to school. These barriers are often experienced in multiples and all pose difficulties that result in low levels of access to mainstream recreation provision. Dedicated provision varies greatly across the country, with Dublin having the best range of recreation provision for young people with disabilities and impairments.

Participation in recreation by people with disabilities has a number of social benefits. People establish friendships and social networks. Participation facilitates social integration, can bridge cultural differences and pave the way to employment. Participation in sport with people who have various levels of ability and disability can help overcome prejudice and discrimination, and can play a role in achieving an inclusive society (*see Boxes 27 and 28*).

Box 27: Special Olympics 2003 in Ireland

The experience of participating in activities and working alongside people with disabilities is a fundamental way of changing prejudices. The Special Olympics 2003 in Ireland provides a case in point. The Games provided an opportunity to change people's outlook towards people with learning disabilities. As the National Disability Authority said in its 2005 report, *Promoting the participation of people with disabilities in physical activity and sport in Ireland*: 'It was the first time the Games were held outside the United States and they provided us with the largest international sporting event in our island's history. There were some 7,000 athletes, 3,000 coaches/delegates and 28,000 families and friends at the Games. It is estimated that over 40,000 international visitors came to Ireland specifically for the Games and that the event brought in the order of €35 million into the Irish economy, as well as placing Ireland in the centre of the world's gaze for ten memorable days in June.'

Source: NDA (2005)

Box 28: Sports for All — Young Social Innovators '06

Students from East Glendalough School, Wicklow, undertook this project (No. 81 in the Young Social Innovators '06 Showcase) with the aim of creating a physical education curriculum for primary and secondary schools that was inclusive of people with disabilities. To help make this a reality, the team, aware that many of the games played in school excluded people with a disability, researched games that could be played by all and tried these out in their own school. Promoting the idea in other schools proved very popular. To cope with the demand generated by their work, the team produced a video as a promotional aid for interested schools. In their own school, more inclusive sports are now part of the annual sports day. Overall, the project created greater awareness of life for people with disabilities, not just in sports.

Access to sport for the disabled

A group of students from Newtown School in Waterford wanted to raise awareness with other schools and the local community of the need for access to sport for people with a disability. As part of the Young Social Innovators '06 Showcase (Project No. 70), the students devised a programme of orienteering for all levels of ability. They also raised funds for Enable Ireland and Waterford Cheshire Homes. They made a wide number of links in the process of their project, including One World Centre, Waterford City Council, Barcelona Project Group, IOA, Irish Wheelchair Association and St. Martin's School for Special Needs. The students hope that their adapted orienteering will help people with disabilities to enjoy physical exercise. They are confident that this start, along with the raised profile of the issue and the connections they have made, can be further developed in the future.

Source: Young Social Innovators (2006)

Availability and access

A number of organisations cater for the recreational needs of young people with disabilities, including:
- Special Olympics Ireland
- Irish Wheelchair Association Sport
- Paralympic Council of Ireland
- Irish Blind Sports
- Irish Deaf Sports Association
- Cerebral Palsy Sports Ireland
- Archery Ireland
- Irish Sailing Association
- Tennis Ireland
- Badminton Union of Ireland
- Cycling Ireland
- Equestrian Federation of Ireland
- National Rifle and Pistol Association of Ireland
- National Federation of Arch Clubs (*see Box 29*)
- Football Association of Ireland (*see Box 29*)

Box 29: Activities for the disabled

The **National Federation of Arch Clubs** aims to promote recreational, leisure and social facilities for people with learning disabilities. It has over 40 clubs nationwide, catering for young people with special needs with the help of adult and young volunteers. These clubs provide a social outlet to fun-filled, friendship clubs for people with special needs. Activities are as typical and as wide-ranging as in any youth club.

Further information: www.archclubs.com

The **Football Association of Ireland** has appointed a full-time Development Officer with specific responsibilities to coordinate the provision of football opportunities for people with disabilities. The 'Football for All' Programme works in partnership with a number of organisations to provide recreational, educational and competitive football opportunities.

Further information: www.fai.ie

Swimming is particularly attractive to people with disabilities since buoyancy in water enhances ease of movement. Swim Ireland, as the national governing body for swimming and associated aquatic disciplines, aims to provide appropriate opportunities to all those who wish to participate in swimming in whatever capacity they choose. Swim Ireland works in partnership with the national governing bodies for disability in Ireland to promote the sport of swimming for all and to coordinate swimming activities with a view to enhancing the efforts of the sport and the swimmers to grow and flourish.

Local authorities are required to provide disabled access to their local public pool facilities and have provided disabled car park spaces and ramp access to buildings. However, standard designs and construction still present considerable obstacles for the use of swimming pools by people with disabilities. For example,

standard changing cubicles are not sufficiently wide to take a wheelchair; wheelchair progress from the changing facilities to the pool is often obstructed by a foot bath; and entry to the pool is invariably by way of a ladder. Relatively small changes in design and construction of these areas could improve access enormously. The Department of Arts, Sport and Tourism is considering how these aspects of access to swimming pools can be enhanced.

A 2005 report by the National Disability Authority, *Promoting the participation of people with disabilities in physical activity and sport in Ireland* (NDA, 2005), makes a number of recommendations, including:

- A National Framework for Inclusive Physical Recreation and Sport should be developed by a multi-agency working group in order to plan and promote cross-disciplinary planning and collaboration in the field of physical activity and sport.
- The media should be more inclusive by developing strategies that allot space to a diversity of sports and should portray images of children and adults with a disability in publicity material on sport and physical activity.
- Guidelines should be issued for teachers of students with disabilities.
- Mandatory modules on inclusive/adaptive physical activity (APA) should be introduced into all relevant third-level courses.
- Disability awareness modules should be included in the education and training of those who deliver the Irish Sports Council's recreation programmes.
- Disability awareness training should be provided or available for staff in childcare facilities and leisure and play settings.
- A nationwide volunteering service for sport and physical activity for people with disabilities should be developed. This could be through the network of Local Sports Partnerships.
- People with a disability could be recruited for training and employment in the field of leisure and sports.

The National Disability Authority has developed a statutory Code of Practice on Accessibility of Public Services and Information provided by Public Bodies under the Disability Act 2005 (NDA, 2006). The Code has been developed in order to support public bodies in fulfilling their statutory obligations under Sections 26, 27 and 28 of the Act. Access to services is one of the core elements of the Code, which states that public bodies must make provision for ensuring that, as far as is practicable and appropriate, all of the services it offers, pursuant to the Act, are provided in an integrated and accessible way.

Actions to support the achievement of Objective 4

Young people in rural areas
- The National Spatial Strategy, the National Rural Development Programme and expenditure under the National Development Plan will have regard to the provision of social and community infrastructure, such as parks, sporting and cultural facilities, that will meet the needs of young people.
- The development of the Sports Facilities Strategy should take account of key issues affecting young people in rural areas and their ability to access facilities.
- The mainstreamed Rural Transport Initiative should specifically address the needs of young people in rural areas to access recreational facilities locally.
- The Department of the Environment, Heritage and Local Government, through the local authorities and the Department of Community, Rural and Gaeltacht Affairs, will examine the feasibility of providing more mobile facilities in rural areas.
- The Department of the Environment, Heritage and Local Government, through the Public Library Service, will examine the feasibility of expanding rural library initiatives for young people in rural areas.

Young people from low-income families

- Local development programmes such as RAPID and CLÁR, as well as Measure C of the Local Development Social Inclusion Programme and LEADER, will identify the potential for actively supporting improved recreation provision for young people within disadvantaged communities, including activities during the summer holidays (in circumstances where they are not already being provided by the local authorities).

Young people who are at risk

- Young people at risk should be consulted and actively involved in projects and programmes designed for them.
- Further research should be carried out on how to motivate young people at risk to engage in positive leisure activities.
- The Office of the Minister for Children will raise with the Department of Community, Rural and Gaeltacht Affairs the feasibility of using Dormant Accounts funding to provide support for activities that have a traditional appeal to youth in disadvantaged areas or at risk.
- The Garda Juvenile Diversion Programme will be expanded to 100 projects in 2007.

Young people from ethnic minority groups

Specific efforts should be made to encourage young people from ethnic minority groups to participate in recreational activities. In particular:

- Boards of Management should be encouraged to make teenagers from ethnic minorities aware of after-school activities and facilitate young people to participate in them.
- The Libraries and Cultural Diversity Project Team will make recommendations on the development of library services for the multicultural society in Ireland.
- The National Consultative Council on Racism and Interculturalism will look specifically at the needs of young people from ethnic minority groups and how these can best be met by existing providers.
- The National Youth Council of Ireland, with the support of the Department of Education and Science, will take the lead in the development of an Intercultural Strategy for the youth work sector.

Young people from the Traveller community

- Further research should be undertaken with young Travellers to determine the extent of discrimination against them when they attempt to engage in mainstream recreation. Issues emerging from the research will be addressed in the National Action Plan against Racism.
- The Department of Education and Science, through the youth work sector, will continue to provide financial assistance to recreational and development projects for young Travellers, including girls.
- The Office of the Minister for Children will include young Travellers in its Children and Young People's Forum, established to advise the Minister on the implementation of the National Children's Strategy.

Young people who are ill

- Hospitals in which adolescent patients are treated will work towards providing an environment that is suitable and adaptable to their recreational needs.
- The implementation of Article 7 of the Charter for Children in Hospital will be specifically addressed in the development of the new Children's Hospital (Department of Health and Children/HSE) and in its ultimate operation (HSE).

Young people with disabilities

• City and County Development Boards should pay particular attention to recruiting young people with disabilities to Comhairle na nÓg.

• Strategies developed for young people's recreation locally should specifically address issues relating to the involvement of young people with disabilities in mainstream recreation.

• Sectoral plans will be implemented by the relevant Government departments to implement Part 3 of the Disability Act 2005, dealing with access to buildings and services.

• The Department of Education and Science should highlight the value of projects such as 'Sport for All' in ensuring that PE programmes in schools are planned and implemented to include students with disabilities.

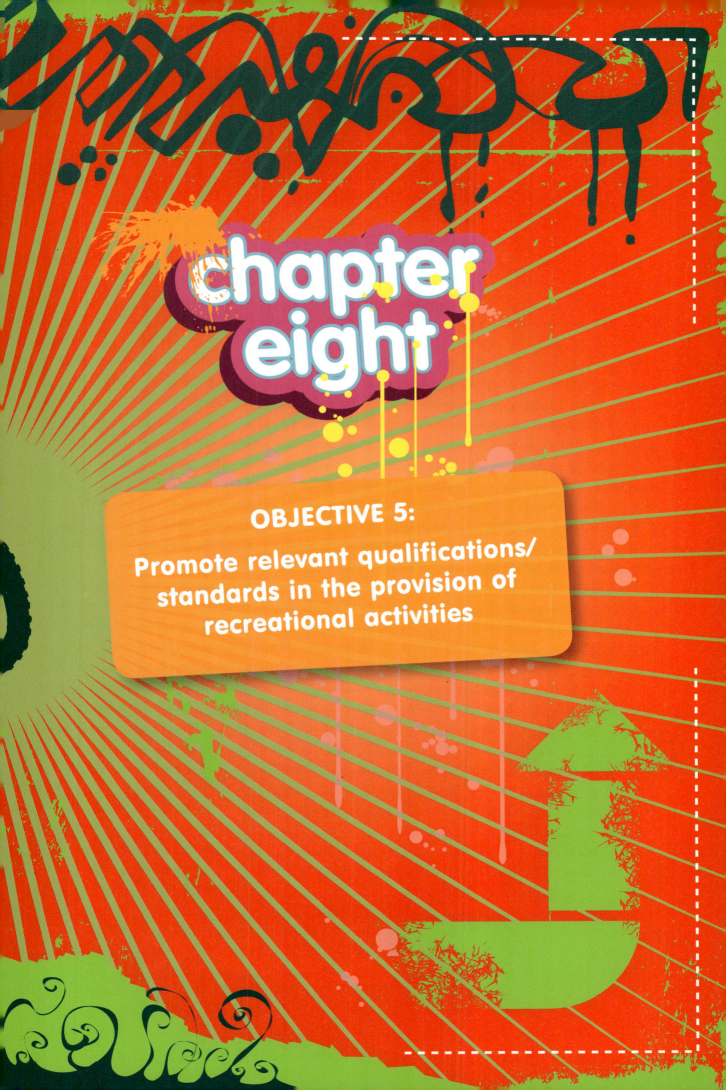

chapter eight

OBJECTIVE 5:

Promote relevant qualifications/standards in the provision of recreational activities

Objective 5 of the National Recreation Policy deals with standards in relation to the quality and safety of recreational facilities used by young people. It also seeks to address issues about the qualifications of people dealing with young people in recreational settings.

During the public consultation for the policy, it emerged that the majority of respondents (93%) agreed with Objective 5, regarding it as being of great importance to screen those who come in contact with children and young people through recreational activities (OMC, 2006). However, a small, but significant number of respondents (7%) had a problem with any attempts to 'over-professionalise' the area of recreation since they felt it could be off-putting to many existing or new volunteers.

The issue is one of balance — between encouraging and retaining adult volunteers and staff working in recreational settings and ensuring that adequate procedures are in place to protect young people while they are engaged in recreation.

Training

Training of staff and volunteers who work with young people is an essential requirement to ensure the success of any programme/initiative. Research and experience would indicate that particular skill sets are necessary for those who are involved with young people. Thus a balance needs to be maintained between ensuring adequate training and yet not over-professionalising the sector. This is recognised in the National Youth Work Development Plan, which states: '*Youth work has thrived throughout its history on the goodwill and voluntary effort of community-spirited individuals … Even in recent years, when more and more paid workers have been employed in youth work, it has often been the case that their demonstrated commitment, interest and record of involvement have been decisive in securing employment rather than specific professional training or qualifications … Such qualities and such people should continue to be rewarded*' (Department of Education and Science, 2003a).

Training is provided for youth work personnel within Ireland as follows:
- Training for voluntary youth leaders in leadership and programme areas, generally provided by youth organisations for new and existing youth leaders within their own organisations.
- Training for members of youth organisations in leadership and programme areas, also generally provided by youth organisations for their own members.
- Pre-Service and In-Service Training for paid youth workers in a variety of areas, provided by youth organisations, universities and other bodies.
- Programme Training for youth leaders and youth workers in particular programme areas, provided by a variety of organisations and bodies.

One of the key actions in the National Youth Work Development Plan was the establishment of a Youth Work Validation Body to develop a comprehensive framework for accreditation and certification in youth work, taking into account the provisions of the Qualifications (Education and Training) Act, 1999 and the need for accessible and flexible progression routes for both volunteers and paid workers. A Committee for the Professional Endorsement of Youth Work Training was established on an all-Ireland basis in October 2005. The committee is responsible for the professional endorsement of courses, programmes of education and training in youth work provided by higher education institutions. The establishment of this committee is an important step in the development of youth work training.

Training in how to work effectively with young people in recreational settings is broader than the youth work sector and includes people working with young people in the sports and community sectors.

Research carried out for the purpose of this policy revealed that 'not liking the leader' was one of the main reasons why young people drop out of activities (De Róiste and Dinneen, 2005). This was evident across a range of activities (*see Table 2*) and suggests that skills in working with young people in recreational settings need to be further developed across all sectors.

Table 2: Reasons for drop-out, by activity

	Dance	Gaelic football	Soccer	Youth club	Music	Scouts/ Guides	Swimming	Martial arts
Did not like the leader	31%	29%	29%	17%	32%	39%	16%	28%

A consistent theme identified during the public consultation for this policy was that young people should be encouraged to take up roles as leaders instead of encouraging qualified adults to do so. Having young people as leaders and facilitators of recreation may also encourage more young people to take part in recreation. As one young person pointed out, '*It's not cool to have it [recreation] run by adults*'. This issue, particularly the involvement of young people in the governance of organisations, has been dealt with under Objective 1 (*see Chapter 4*). Adequate support and training needs to be provided to enable young people to take up roles as leaders in clubs and organisations (*see Box 30*).

> **Box 30: Youth Work Ireland**
>
> Youth Work Ireland has published *A Guide to Quality Standards in Youth Services*, which advises that each youth service should have clear policy and procedures in place to facilitate ongoing training and development for young people, staff and volunteers.
>
> *Source*: Youth Work Ireland (2004)

Working out of hours

One of the most significant issues identified by young people in the research conducted for this policy was the need for somewhere to hang out in the evening time, after school, during holidays and at weekends (De Róiste and Dinneen, 2005). Thus, it is clear that working with young people in their free time requires a commitment to work outside of normal office hours. For example, the key facilities that young people identified (such as youth cafés and drop-in centres) would be required to be open at night, particularly at weekends. This is a key issue that needs to be recognised in the contracts of those working with young people.

Child protection and welfare

The Government has guidelines for the protection of children and young people concerned with keeping them safe and ensuring best practice among those who work with them. The key documents are:
- *Children First: National Guidelines for the Protection and Welfare of Children*, published by the Department of Health and Children (1999).
- *Our Duty to Care: The principles of good practice for the protection of children and young people*, also published by the Department of Health and Children (2002) and aimed at community and voluntary organisations of any size or type that provide services for children and young people.

The *Children First* guidelines state that all organisations providing services to children and young people have a responsibility to:

- promote the general welfare, health, development and safety of children;
- adopt and consistently apply a safe and clearly defined method of recruiting and selecting staff and volunteers;
- raise awareness within the organisation about potential risks to children's safety and welfare;
- develop effective screening procedures for responding to accidents and complaints;
- develop procedures to provide specific guidance to staff and volunteers who may have reasonable grounds for concern about the safety and welfare of children involved with the organisation;
- identify a designated person to act as a liaison with external agencies and as a resource person to any staff member or volunteer who has child protection concerns.

There are also codes of practice for the youth work sector (Department of Education and Science, 2003b), the sports sector (Irish Sports Council and Sports Council for Northern Ireland, 2006) and the arts sector (Arts Council, 2006).

Training and awareness of child protection issues are provided by the Health Service Executive (HSE). In the youth work sector, these issues are the responsibility of a National Coordinator for Child Protection, appointed by the National Youth Council of Ireland in 2004 to implement their 2002 code. Within the sports sector, training is provided by the Irish Sports Council in conjunction with the HSE.

While progress has been made in implementing the *Children First* guidelines, a number of challenges remain for their full implementation. One of the challenges in protecting young people in a recreational setting is the variety in the level of awareness among voluntary organisations and community groups, as well as limited awareness among children, young people and their parents of the objectives and requirements of *Children First*, particularly within clubs, church- and community-based organisations (National Children's Advisory Council, 2002). The Government, through the Office of the Minister for Children, is currently undertaking a review of the operation of the *Children First* guidelines.

Criminal history vetting

A related issue is the criminal history vetting of people dealing with young people in recreational settings. At present, staff in a wide range of public sector facilities involving access to children are not vetted. This includes staff in leisure centres, public libraries and park wardens.

The Government has clearly recognised the importance of the criminal history vetting of individuals coming into contact with young people, while noting that such checks are not the sole answer to ensuring applicants' suitability for posts.

The Report of the Working Group on Garda Vetting was published in 2004, setting out a comprehensive national strategy for a major expansion in Garda vetting arrangements (Department of Justice, Equality and Law Reform, 2004). This strategy envisages that all organisations that recruit and select people who would have substantial, unsupervised access to children and vulnerable adults should avail of — and should be entitled to avail of — the vetting services of the Garda Central Vetting Unit (GCVU).

A multi-agency Implementation Group on Garda Vetting continues to progress implementation of the recommendations of the Report of the Working Group, which deal with human and financial resource requirements, work processes and legal issues.

The implementation of measures to allow expansion in the vetting service of the Garda Síochána is continuing. Substantial additional staff have already been provided to the GCVU and significant changes have been made in work processes in order to streamline the vetting application process. These developments allowed the commencement of the phased expansion of vetting services in the first quarter of 2006.

This phased expansion is proceeding in a planned and structured manner in consultation with Government departments responsible for the care of children and vulnerable adults. It will continue until vetting is available in respect of all people working in a full-time, part-time or voluntary capacity with children or vulnerable adults (subject to compliance with administrative regulations), irrespective of the employment sector.

Proportionate protection

While young people need to be protected when they are engaging in recreation, issues arise if child protection requirements result in the curtailment of recreational opportunities available to young people.

Scotland's Commissioner for Children and Young People (2006) has chosen 'Promoting Proportionate Protection' as her policy priority for the next two years. This policy will look at the issue of over-protection of children and young people since many respondents to a public consultation undertaken by her Office stressed the need to balance appropriate protection with fun, adventure and healthy relationships. Organisations that were consulted mentioned missed opportunities for play and adventure for children and the imbalance between risk and challenge.

Several examples were given of situations in which the balance between protection and appropriate risk or support was wrong. This resulted in:
- play opportunities and outdoor experiences being curtailed;
- not enough attention being given to the positive benefits of risk and challenge;
- vetting/disclosure processes that are cumbersome and put people off working with children and young people;
- a shortage of people working with children and young people because of fears of allegations.

The Scottish experience highlights the importance of achieving the correct balance between protection and affording young people the opportunity to participate in fun activities.

Technology issues related to the protection of young people

The evidence has shown that young people are using technology to a greater extent than ever before. This includes computer technology and mobile phones. The pace at which young people adopt new technology steadily increases between the ages of 10-14 (Internet Advisory Board, 2005). New technology, such as the Internet (e.g. websites, e-mail, newsgroups, chat rooms), carries risks particularly for young users. Adequate supervision by parents is the best way to protect teenagers from exposure to these risks while respecting the young person's privacy. Research has found that while the majority of parents (83%) discuss the potential dangers of using the Internet with their child, this declines as children reach 13-14 years of age.

The Internet Advisory Board advises parents of steps they can take to ensure their children are protected while using the Internet. The Board has produced a parents' guide, *Get With IT*, which is designed to make parents more aware of how the new media works and encourage them to engage with, and use, new technologies with their children. The guide gives details on all new media technologies, including digital TV, the Internet, mobile phones and interactive game consoles. It also gives advice on how to recognise if a child is using new media technologies in a potentially dangerous way and what steps a parent can take to prevent or stop this.

Those public libraries that provide Internet access to young people have policies in place to ensure that such access is appropriately monitored and supervised.

The National Centre for Technology in Education (NCTE) promotes the safe and responsible use of the Internet in collaboration with schools and parents' councils. Safety information leaflets have been distributed to children in schools and are available in community centres and libraries as part of the 'Be Wise on the Net Campaign' (NCTE, 2002). The NCTE has been working with the Office of the Minister for Children on this issue.

Mobile phones

Research undertaken for this policy shows a clear rise in the number of teenagers who own mobile phones, rising from 87% of 12-year-olds to 97.5% of 17-year-olds to 100% ownership by 18-year-olds (De Róiste and Dinneen, 2005).

While mobile phones offer reassurance to parents that they can contact their children at all times (and vice versa), there are potentially the same kinds of dangers associated with mobile phones as with the Internet, including unwanted images or contact.

The Irish Cellular Industry Association (ICIA) has done work in the area of safe and responsible use of mobile phones. In 2005, the ICIA published *A Parents' Guide to Mobile Phones*, which seeks to educate parents and guardians in the ways in which they can gain greater visibility of their child's mobile usage and the services they access. It also highlights the facility provided by operators, which allows authorised access for parents to a child's account.

The ICIA Code of Practice has recently been revised to take account of the advances in mobile phones technology and includes reasonable and proportionate measures to be taken by operators to ensure that inappropriate content is neither made available to minors nor is a cause for offence to the public in general (Irish Cellular Industry Association, 2006).

Audiovisual media services

With over 99% of the population in possession of television sets, the influence of television on everyday life in Ireland is beyond doubt. As a consequence, the regulation of the broadcasting sector continues to be of prime importance given the impact of that sector on society in general and as a source of recreation for young people.

The Broadcasting Commission of Ireland (BCI) is the independent statutory organisation responsible for a number of key areas of activity with regard to the television and radio sectors in Ireland, including the development of codes and rules in relation to programming and advertisement standards. The BCI has developed a Children's Advertising Code (Broadcasting) under Section 19 of the Broadcasting Act 2001, which specifies standards to be complied with and rules and practices to be observed on advertising that is likely to be of direct or indirect interest to children (BCI, 2004). The Code became fully operational in January 2005 and applies to all Irish broadcasting services.

Safety standards for recreation

Youth, community and sports centres funded by the State are required to comply with building regulations (*see Box 31*). Swimming pools are required to comply with water quality standards and they are also subject to inspections by the Health and Safety Authority.

> **Box 31: Operational standards for youth, community and sports centres**
>
> There has been considerable investment in multi-use facilities in recent years for communities and for youth at risk in particular. Dublin City Council (2004) has published a manual entitled *Operational Standards for Dublin City Council-run Youth, Community and Sports Centres*, in which it was recognised that there needs to be a professional, safe and youth-centred needs approach with regard to the delivery of activities and programmes.
>
> The manual focuses on the policy and procedure needed to deal with the following objectives:
>
> - The criteria and conditions of funding from Government on facilities aimed at improving services for young people at risk of drug use and providing alternative strategies for other development.
>
> - The defining of roles and responsibilities of Dublin City Council and its staff, advisory committees, end-users and all other stakeholders in each of its centres.
>
> - Ensuring the facilities/centres are run in an efficient and professional manner so as to provide as many opportunities as possible for the target groups and wider community.
>
> - Ensuring the facilities are constructed and operated to the highest health and safety standards, guaranteeing access to all sectors of society.
>
> - To promote a joined-up approach to providing youth services, sports and recreation, and community resources under one roof in a multi-use facility.
>
> *Source*: Dublin City Council (2004)

Many commercial swimming pools and leisure centres are members of the Institute of Leisure and Amenity Management (ILAM), the professional body for the leisure industry in Ireland. ILAM is an independent national organisation, operating on a non-profit basis and with voluntary membership. It operates a 'White Flag' award scheme, which is primarily a hygiene and environmental award with a number of key criteria, falling under the following broad headings: facility exterior and ground; swimming pools hygiene; environmental management; water quality and treatment; facility interior; operations; and education and information.

A number of pools and leisure centres run by local authorities, which are members of ILAM, received White Flag awards in 2005.

Maintenance of facilities

In some cases where funding has been provided for capital expenditure, it has been difficult to secure funding on an ongoing basis for other costs, such as maintenance. There are issues regarding the ongoing maintenance and repair of facilities that are under the control of individual groups (e.g. scout dens) as well as community facilities. While the initial capital may be provided for the facility, there are few grants available for the ongoing maintenance and renovation of these buildings, which results in their becoming run-down over time. This, in turn, has implications for the attractiveness of these as venues for young people, as well as for the wider community.

Specific provision for current and administration costs has been made by some funds, such as the Young People's Facilities and Services Fund (YPFSF) which provides funding towards the cost of youth workers and centre managers, and a contribution to the running costs of youth centres developed under the YPFSF.

In April 2006, the Minister for the Environment, Heritage and Local Government announced a new capital fund for the development of local social and community facilities. This scheme funds targeted capital developments, carried out through local authorities, that are designed to enhance communities, address disadvantage and improve social cohesion at a local level. It includes upgrading community, cultural and sports facilities.

Insurance

In the case of buildings and play and recreation facilities, public bodies, including local authorities, can avail of insurance provided by the Irish Public Bodies Mutual Insurance (IPBMI) Ltd, a statutory non-profit-making body. Groups in the youth work sector carry their own insurance, which is also applied to their premises. The cost of insuring buildings can be prohibitive for community groups, which rely on commercial insurance cover. It is easier for community groups to obtain public liability insurance to run particular projects, such as summer projects, since local authorities provide small grants to cover items including insurance.

Young people, especially teenagers, enjoy challenging and adventurous activities, such as abseiling, canoeing, scuba diving and horse riding, all of which involve some element of risk. It would appear, however, that it is increasingly difficult for young people to participate in such organised adventure activities due to the difficulties in securing insurance. This emerged as a significant issue in discussions undertaken as part of formulating this policy. The National Play Policy recognised that there should be a trade-off between the desire of young people to have exciting and challenging play (or recreation) opportunities, involving a degree of risk, and concerns about the need to protect children and young people in public spaces.

Risk can be reduced by taking account of factors that may result in accident, injury claims or negligence. Establishing relevant standards can assist in minimising risk and in protecting both the participants and the service provider.

Many of the more adventurous activities, popular with young people, where insurance is an issue are covered by the Adventure Activities Standards Authority Act 2001. The functions of the Authority under the Act are to promote, encourage, foster, facilitate and regulate the safe operation of adventure activities in the State. Other functions of the Authority are to establish a register of all adventure activities operators and to prepare and publish codes of practice for the purpose of providing practical guidance on the safe operation of each of the 13 specified adventure activities. The activities encompassed by the Act are hill-walking in areas more than 300 metres above sea level; orienteering in areas more than 300 metres above sea level; caving; dinghy sailing; kayaking; canoeing; surfing with a surf board; wind surfing; scuba diving; snorkeling; abseiling; archery; and rock climbing.

In view of the lapse of time since the passage of the Adventure Activity Standards Authority Act 2001 (which has not yet commenced) and recent proposed developments in relation to maritime safety structures, the Department of Transport is establishing an interdepartmental/agency working group to examine options for how best to proceed on this issue. The group comprises representatives of the Departments of Transport, and of Arts, Sport and Tourism, together with the Irish Sports Council and Fáilte Ireland. It is expected that a report of the deliberations of the group will be submitted to Government by Summer 2007.

There are also a number of initiatives being undertaken to reduce the cost of insurance, including the insurance reform programme being driven by the Department of Enterprise, Trade and Employment. In addition, the establishment of the Personal Injuries Assessment Board should reduce the cost of insurance, including public liability insurance.

Other safety organisations

There are a number of other organisations with a specific role in promoting safety in recreational settings. These include Irish Water Safety, which is the statutory body established to promote water safety in Ireland. The Department of Transport, through the Maritime Safety Directorate and the Irish Coast Guard, is the national authority with responsibility for, among other things, the promotion, regulation and enforcement of maritime safety on vessels. The main focus is on accident prevention through an appropriate combination of regulation and heightening of safety awareness and enforcement.

Equipment

It is important that equipment used by young people while engaging in recreation conforms to recognised standards. Limiting damage caused by vandalism can also reduce the likelihood of negligence claims.

Public bodies, including local authorities, can avail of insurance provided by the Irish Public Bodies Mutual Insurance (IPBMI) for equipment provided in public play and recreation facilities, providing it conforms to recognised standards. In addition to conforming with recognised standards, the IPBMI also recommends educating young people who will use the equipment on safety use.

Safety issues can arise with individual items of equipment. The National Standards Authority of Ireland has established a committee to examine the issue of goalpost safety, following the death of a young boy at a soccer camp in August 2004. It is expected that new standards in this area will be made available in 2007. The committee is made up of representatives from the Departments of Arts, Sport and Tourism, and of Education and Science, together with the national governing bodies of sport, manufacturers and technicians. The work of the committee covers three areas:

- technical specifications for goalposts;
- code of practice for procurement, installation, inspection and maintenance of goalposts;
- roll-out of education and safety training.

In the meanwhile, the Football Association of Ireland issued a leaflet on *Goalpost Safety*, which is designed to offer practical guidance towards protecting players' safety.

Actions to support the achievement of Objective 5

- The Health Service Executive will provide a web page on its website designed for young people, parents and the community and voluntary sectors with information on child protection and the requirements of the *Children First* guidelines. A link to this will be provided by the Office of the Minister for Children and the National Play Resource Centre.

- The obstacles to the vetting of people having substantial, unsupervised access to young people in recreational settings will be removed by the ongoing phased implementation of the Report of the Working Group on Garda Vetting.

- The Minister for Justice, Equality and Law Reform will continue to explore proposals for legislation to regularise criminal history vetting.

- The Department of Transport will put in place the Adventure Activities Standards Authority, or assign the functions to another appropriate body, to regulate adventure activities.

- Related to the issue of drop-out from activities, publicly funded organisations working with young people in the youth work sector, the sports sector and the arts sector will continue to make arrangements to ensure that both staff and volunteers receive appropriate training in working with young people in recreational settings.

- Youth organisations will be encouraged to ensure that contracts for staff working with young people reflect any out-of-hours requirements of the job.

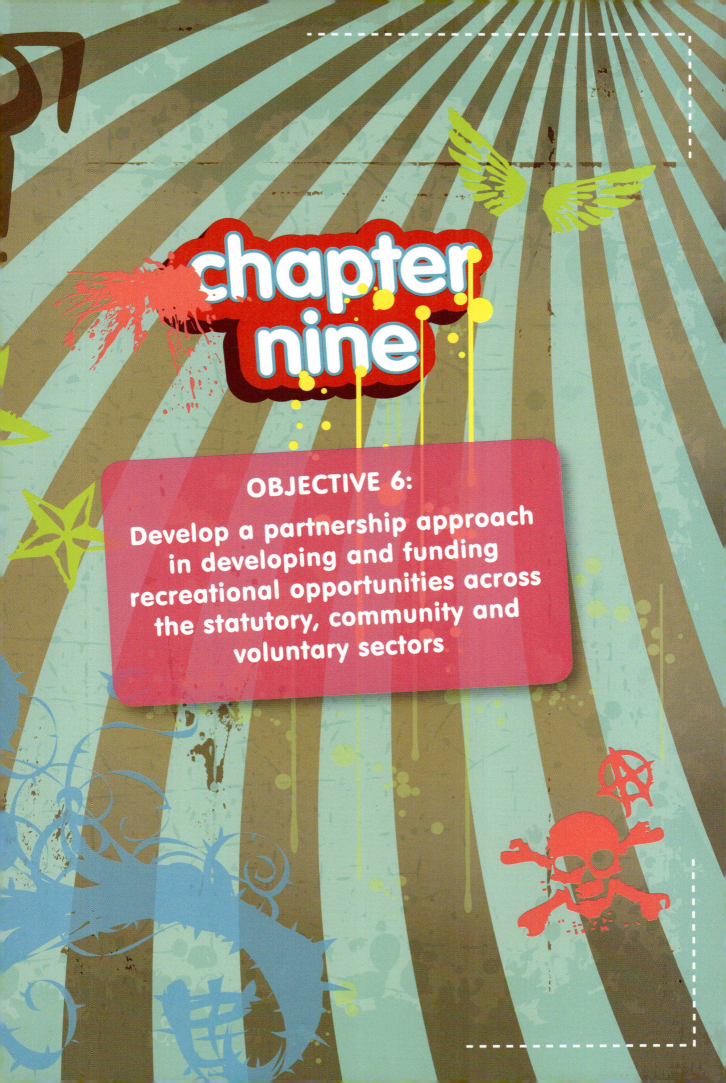

chapter nine

OBJECTIVE 6:

Develop a partnership approach in developing and funding recreational opportunities across the statutory, community and voluntary sectors

The original impetus for addressing partnership on children's issues came from the National Children's Strategy, which recognised the large number of statutory and voluntary agencies involved at both national and local level in the delivery of services for children (Department of Health and Children, 2000a). The strategy outlined the case for child-focused, needs-driven supports and services, and in particular the importance of finding better ways to link services.

The framework for implementing the National Children's Strategy, the 'Engine for Change', was designed to achieve more effective collaboration between Government, its departments, statutory agencies and voluntary service providers in identifying and addressing children's needs. It sets out a framework of support designed to facilitate more effective cooperation between these various sectors.

In order to support integrated planning and service delivery for children at local level, City and County Development Boards (quadripartite parties from local government, local development agencies, the State sector and social partners) were assigned particular responsibilities to identify gaps and overlaps in service provision and to secure coherent delivery arrangements by agencies operating locally.

To build on the progress achieved to date in the implementation of the goals of the National Children's Strategy, the main objectives in formulating the National Recreation Policy were:
- To explore partnership approaches using existing structures, with the emphasis on maximising interagency cooperation/coordination, avoiding duplication and ensuring shared quality standards.
- To examine the important contribution that parents and families, as well as the wider community and young people themselves, can make to the development of recreational opportunities.
- To examine issues concerning the funding of public recreational facilities and programmes to ensure that provision matches need, as well as the scope for private investment in the expansion of recreational opportunities for young people.

In the public consultation undertaken as part of the process of developing this policy, 757 respondents (95%) agreed with the objective of developing a partnership approach to the development and funding of recreational opportunities for young people, while 38 respondents (5%) considered that such an approach could be difficult to implement and sustain (OMC, 2006). The need for more integration between the sectors involved in providing recreational activities was identified as an issue.

Role of Government departments and agencies

At national level, there is no single Government department responsible for the provision of recreational programmes and facilities for young people. Responsibility rests with a number of different Government departments and statutory agencies. Many of the programmes funded by these have different objectives and are designed to meet the requirements of different client groups.

Figure 2 shows the main Government departments and agencies that provide recreational and leisure facilities for young people and identifies the structures in place at national, regional and local level for the delivery of programmes and initiatives. Details of the role and functions of Government departments and agencies are set out in Appendix 1.

Figure 2: Structures in place for provision of recreation facilities and related activities

Arts, Sport and Tourism		Education and Science	Community, Rural and Gaeltacht Affairs	Health and Children	Justice, Equality and Law Reform	Environment, Heritage and Local Government	
National Cultural Institutions	Irish Sports Council	Vocational Education Committees (VECs)	Regional Drugs Task Forces	Health Service Executive (HSE)	An Garda Síochána	Local Authorities (LAs)	City and County Development Boards
	Local Sports Partnerships	Staff	Local Drugs Task Forces	Health Promotion Officers	Garda Juvenile Diversion Programme	Play/Arts/ Sport/ Officers	LAs
	VECs	Parents				Libraries	LDSIPs
	LAs	LAs	Local Development Groups	Physical Activity Coordinators		Community Amenity/ Recreation	LEADER
	HSE	+ 4 from:					CEBs
	FÁS	Students					Gardaí
	NGBs	College Trustees					Dept. CR & GA
	Universities	VECs					Dept. Ed & Sc
	Colleges	Commercial					Dept. S & FA
	Institutes	Irish language interests					VECs
	Commercial sports clubs	Community/ Voluntary groups					Enterprise Ireland
	Voluntary/ Community groups						FÁS
							HSE
							Childcare Cmt.
							IDA
							Regional Tourism Authority
							Teagasc
							Udaras na Gael.
							Empl/Business
							Voluntary & Community
							Agri. & Farming
							Trade unions
							+ Sectoral

At local level, the Local Government Act 2001 provides broad discretionary powers for a local authority to take such measures and engage in activities (including the incurring of expenditure) as it considers necessary or desirable to promote the interests of the local community, including the support of amenity, sport and recreational facilities. A range of other structures also exist at local level and play an important role in providing recreation programmes for young people, including City and County Development Boards, the Health Service Executive, VECs, Local Sports Partnerships and Local Drugs Task Forces. In addition and most importantly, the recreation needs of young people could not be met without the very significant contribution made by the voluntary and community sectors.

Funding structures

Ireland is unusual in the extent to which recreational programmes and facilities are funded by central government but managed locally. Elsewhere, it would appear that primary responsibility rests with local authorities.

Different funding streams, as well as the wide variety of organisations through which funding is channelled, present challenges for the coordination of service delivery locally. The complexity of funding arrangements at local level and the difficulty in establishing the funding streams is a much wider issue than recreational facilities for young people. In 2002, Waterford City Council's Social Inclusion Unit carried out an exercise in tracking expenditure under social inclusion measures under the National Development Plan in the Waterford area. Following from that exercise, a number of Government departments and agencies (Environment, Heritage and Local Government; Education and Science; Community, Rural and Gaeltacht Affairs; and the Health Service Executive, in conjunction with Waterford City and County Development Boards) have developed a pilot project to track expenditure in relation to early school-leavers and youth at risk. The objective of this exercise is to maximise the impact of resources and to help fill gaps in services with a better outcome for this particular target group. This exercise is not yet completed, but it could provide a model, suitably adapted, in other areas.

Improved coordination at central and local level

Both central and local government need to develop more effective partnerships to provide and fund recreational and leisure facilities and to coordinate and integrate more effectively the arrangements for the implementation and delivery of individual programmes. Many of the most successful examples of recreation illustrated in this policy (see *tinted boxes*) highlight the effectiveness of partnerships at local level.

Public service providers, including Government departments, need to adopt a more integrated and coordinated approach towards the provision of services and facilities for young people. There are examples of effective interagency cooperation. For example, the Department of Arts, Sport and Tourism works with the Irish Sports Council in determining priorities at national and regional level. It also works with the Department of Community, Rural and Gaeltacht Affairs in the administration of the Sports Capital and RAPID Programmes, particularly in areas of disadvantage.

One of the key issues emerging in discussions during the preparation of this policy is the need for a mechanism for decision-making at central government level to be informed by local knowledge. This should result in improved targeting of resources and more sustainable programmes. This happens with some programmes. In the case of the Young People's Facilities and Services Fund, for example, plans are developed by local development groups (consisting of representatives of the Local Drugs Task Force, the local VEC and the relevant local authority), with a wide-ranging canvas of the local community being

undertaken before plans are finalised. In general, however, mechanisms for the involvement of agencies with local knowledge in central government decision-making are underdeveloped.

City and County Development Boards were established in 2000 to bring about a more coordinated delivery of public and local development services at local level. A core function of the Boards was to draw up and oversee the implementation of an agreed strategy for the economic, social and cultural development of their counties and cities. The City and County Development Board structure will be developed and strengthened under the new Social Partnership Agreement, *Towards 2016*, as a vehicle for supporting a more integrated approach to service delivery at local level (Department of the Taoiseach, 2006).

The City and County Development Boards have a role in the implementation of the National Children's Strategy. They have also incorporated play and recreation in their Strategies for Economic and Social Development. Under the Lifecycle Framework of the new Social Partnership Agreement, a new multi-agency Children's Committee will be established within each City and County Development Board, to be chaired by the Health Service Executive. These committees will be well placed to develop local recreation strategies and thus bring a strategic approach to the development of recreation opportunities for young people within their areas.

A key element in a strategic approach to developing recreation facilities is to establish what exists at present and then to identify the gaps. In some cases, this can be easily done; for example, it is relatively easy to identify local authority swimming pools and public libraries and facilities provided under the Young People's Facilities and Services Fund.

A more complete picture of youth work activity at local level will be facilitated by the further implementation of the Youth Work Act 2001 when VECs will be required to develop youth work development plans (*see below*). It is more difficult in other areas such as sporting facilities. The Department of Arts, Sport and Tourism is in the process of developing a Sports Facilities Strategy. This aims at a planned approach to the development of sports facilities that will engage people in sports participation at all levels. One of the objectives of this strategy will be to complete an audit of sports facilities to help determine priorities for future development. These developments should contribute to a more complete picture of facilities locally.

Strategic planning at local level will also be assisted by the further implementation of the Youth Work Act 2001, which will take place in 2006 and allow for improved local coordination of youth work services. Vocational Education Committees (VECs) will have responsibility for the preparation and implementation of 3-year Youth Work Development Plans for each VEC area (while ensuring coordination of youth work with other services for young people). A Youth Work Committee will be established to advise and make recommendations to each VEC on the performance of its youth work functions. Voluntary Youth Councils will also be established in each VEC area to advise on matters related to the Youth Work Development Plan and to act as a forum for voluntary youth work organisations operating in the VEC area. An Assessor of Youth Work will be appointed who will support the development of good youth work practices through the assessment, monitoring and review of youth work programmes.

There needs to be close cooperation between the VECs and City and County Development Boards in strategic planning for young people at local level.

Action programme at community level

The State sector cannot exclusively provide the means by which young people can pursue leisure and recreational pursuits. Voluntary and community groups, organisations and individuals, including parents and young people, are ideally positioned to bring about positive change in this area. They can play a crucial

role by working in collaboration with each other to build effective partnership arrangements that will have a lasting impact on developing sustainable opportunities and initiatives specifically tailored to respond to their individualised needs at local level and to overcoming barriers to participation.

A community working together can identify, develop and implement well-targeted strategies and initiatives that will maximise the opportunities available to provide recreational opportunities and facilities. The example given in Box 32 illustrates what can be achieved by a community in adopting a proactive approach to identifying suitable and worthwhile opportunities through which the quality of life for its young people can be improved.

Box 32: Thurles Recreation Youth Partnership

In January 2005, two teenagers and their parents decided that, although there were a number of sporting activities in the town of Thurles and a very dynamic young people's musical group (named Phoenix Productions), there were not enough opportunities for young people to just socialise and be with each other. They decided to form a group that would include young people, parents and others in a position to do something to help. A group was formed and the first meeting took place in March 2005. The group included:

- parents with teenage children;
- young people aged 13-18;
- teachers who represented each of the four post-primary schools in the town;
- local representatives, including political representatives, clergy, Gardaí and Town Council.

It was agreed that young people should have a voice in what would take place and that they would be equal partners in the recreation group.

Actions undertaken

1. **Survey of young people's recreational needs**
   A survey of 704 young people attending post-primary school in Thurles was carried out. The findings showed that many young people were unhappy with the number of things to do with their free time and with the number of places to go. They said they wanted the following to be provided: (1) a place to hang out; (2) a leisure centre, (3) clubs; (4) some indoor and outdoor activities; and (5) discos.

   Key success factors in this activity were:
   - having someone with research experience;
   - having a teacher in each school to coordinate the data collection;
   - including young people in drawing up the questionnaire and in helping to code and analyse the results;
   - getting the young people to present the findings in different forums.

2. **Raising awareness**
   When the survey was completed, a meeting was held for people involved in recreational activities for young people in the town. More than 50 people attended and showed great interest in the findings of the survey. Some clubs and organisations identified problems in recruiting young members, while others indicated that they had difficulties in getting volunteers. The survey findings were also presented to the Rotary Club and a leaflet outlining the main findings was developed for young people.

Box 32 *(continued)*

Key success factors in this activity were:
- having a good source of information in the form of a booklet, originally compiled by a parish group, which listed all the relevant organisations operating in Thurles;
- giving clubs and organisations an opportunity to come together for the first time;
- using the findings from the survey as a basis for discussion.

3. No Name Club

It was decided that a No Name Club would be able to meet some of the needs of the young people in Thurles. One parent in the group agreed to lead on this action. An initial disco was held in December and others have taken place since. A number of other activities are also being planned in conjunction with national organisations, including taking part in the national variety show, attendance at the youth awards, involvement in the St. Patrick's Day Parade and visiting other clubs.

Key success factors in this activity were:
- committed parents and young people;
- support from the local hotel to hold the discos;
- involvement of the local Garda Liaison Officer in the No Name Club.

4. Foróige Club

A Foróige club was set up in December 2005 and now has 40 members, all aged 13-14. A number of different activities have already been run, including indoor soccer, dance classes, multicultural arts and crafts classes, and group outings to the cinema and other venues.

Key success factors in this activity were:
- having a committed parent willing to lead;
- support from the Foróige Regional Youth Officer, who provided some training and also back-up support;
- good team of leaders who work on a rota basis (12 at present).

Place to hang out

Tipperary Regional Youth Service, with an office in Thurles, was contacted with a view to developing a place where young people can hang out. This work is being progressed and also involves young people from the No Name Club assisting in the development.

5. Coordinating activities

Initially, it was thought that there were not enough clubs for young people in the town. But following two meetings held with local clubs, it transpired that quantity was not the problem, but rather people knowing about the clubs and the clubs themselves getting recruits and volunteers. The group now sees a role in facilitating a 'recreation fair' in which clubs and organisations can come together with young people to facilitate and promote membership.

Moving forward

The ad hoc group that initiated this project has now formalised its arrangements and officers and committee members (including young people) have been appointed. The group now also includes two additional members from the clubs and organisations with an interest in

Box 32 *(continued)*

young people. A Constitution has also been drawn up. It is expected that the group will continue to develop partnerships with other organisations with an interest in young people so that recreational provision for young people can continue to be developed.

Further information: Thurles Action for Community Development Ltd (tacd@eircom.net)

Local communities can also strengthen their organisational capacities and increase their effectiveness in developing programmes geared towards young people through their active participation and engagement in local partnerships, such as the City and County Development Boards. The active representation and participation by community and voluntary organisations in these Boards will ensure that they have a voice. It also provides a mechanism whereby they can have an input into the provision of youth-centred activities.

Partnerships with young people

Partnerships with young people in the development of recreational opportunities are an important part of the National Recreation Policy. Young people have already taken the initiative in tackling the lack of recreation facilities locally. There are a number of examples of groups of young people identifying a need and then setting about working with local groups to address the issue (*see Boxes 33 and 34*).

Box 33: Winner of the Irish Youth Foundation Award 2005

After highlighting youth concerns in Castlebar, Co. Mayo, the aim of the project was to campaign for a youth centre in the town. Through a local group called Open Space, the students of Davitt College became involved in a feasibility study for the youth centre. They also invited guest speakers to their school and held a Youth Forum, attended by students from three local post-primary schools. They conducted a youth survey and campaigned through their local radio station and in the school newsletter.

In March 2006, the students made a presentation of their proposed solutions at the launch of the feasibility study. Following this, they were approached by the St. Vincent de Paul Society with the offer of a temporary space for the youth centre while a more permanent solution was sought.

The youth centre opened in Castlebar in the summer of 2006. The project team, together with students from the other second-level schools participating, undertook various fundraising activities to purchase furniture and equipment for the youth centre. Located in the V de P premises, the space consists of two rooms — a 'chill-out zone' and a 'games room'. Currently, it is open two nights a week, extending to four nights a week during the mid-term break.

Source: *The Irish Times*, 10 May 2006

Box 34: Teen Builders, not Teen Bingers — Young Social Innovators '06

The purpose of this Young Social Innovators project (No. 133) was to create awareness and educate people about the dangers of drug and alcohol abuse. The students of St. Aloysius College, Carrigtwohill, Co. Cork, researched this issue in their community and on the Internet. They contacted the Gardaí and the Garda Drugs Squad came to their school to give a talk on the dangers of drug abuse. The students also made contact with a wide range of people in the community, including teens, parents, the County Council, youth centres and local clubs, as well as Tabor Lodge. They organised the making of a DVD on anti-social behaviour. They planned to have an Open Morning in April called 'Get Up and Go', to encourage young people to utilise the resources available to them in the community. To coincide with this meeting, they were planning to publish a booklet called *Whaz Hapnen* (*see Box 36*).

Source: Young Social Innovators (2006)

The corporate sector

In addition to the efforts of people at central, local and community level, there is also scope for corporate involvement in expanding recreational opportunities for young people. At EU level, Corporate Social Responsibility (CSR) has been defined as '*a concept whereby companies integrate social and environmental concerns in their business operation and in their interaction with their stakeholders on a voluntary basis*'. CSR aims to integrate companies in their local setting, recognising that they are dependent on the health, stability and prosperity of the communities in which they operate. There are also competitive benefits to the company arising from its contribution locally.

An increasing number of companies in Ireland are embracing the culture of CSR. The Foundation for Investing in Communities reflects this trend, as does the private organisation Business in the Community – Ireland. This latter organisation operates a model that involves a move away from giving money to ad hoc causes to combining corporate giving, skills transfer and resource allocation into one programme, targeting an identified social need (*see Box 35*). An important element of this model is in enabling staff to devote time and skills to areas of identified community need.

Box 35: Business in the Community – Ireland

This organisation has been working closely with companies in order to increase their involvement in volunteering. It considers that it is in the long-term interest of businesses to promote volunteering in their communities. It played an important role, for example, in encouraging companies to allow their staff to volunteer for the 2003 Special Olympics (*see Box 27*).

A number of companies continues to encourage staff to volunteer in the local community, including in some cases in partnerships with youth organisations. Activities include weekly sports and group work activities, summer projects and trips. Companies also use their specific expertise (e.g. in IT) to help young people — in a hands-on, fun environment — who may not otherwise have the opportunity of gaining access to high-tech equipment.

Further information: www.bitc.ie

The drive towards increased levels of social responsibility in the form of corporate community involvement is a viable means of promoting improved recreational and personal development opportunities for young people locally.

Better use of existing facilities

It is important to maximise existing facilities to provide recreational opportunities for young people. These facilities can range from schools to community centres. In addition to the curriculum, most schools provide students with further opportunities through extra-curricular programmes for sport. Outside of sport, school buildings could also be a valuable resource for many of the other activities covered by this policy, particularly in rural areas. This resource could be especially valuable during the holidays when the school is not in use. While the Department of Education and Science has actively encouraged school management to make school facilities available for community use outside of school hours, it is ultimately a matter for school authorities to sanction their use. There has been very little progress on this proposal to date, perhaps because of the ongoing operational costs associated with making schools available (e.g. insurance, heat, light, cleaning and maintenance) and at present it is not possible to meet these costs from within the Department's Vote.

As part of the new school planning model, the Department of Education and Science is collaborating with local authorities to explore the possibility of providing shared school and community facilities on new school campuses. This is likely to feature where new schools are developed over the coming years, particularly in rapidly developing areas of high population density. The Department is working in close partnership with Fingal County Council in relation to the development of community facilities as part of the provision of school buildings. It is important that appropriate mechanisms are put in place to ensure that these facilities are available to the local community, including young people.

Community centres, community halls and other community facilities in the cities, towns and villages across the country are also a valuable complementary resource which have played a significant role in the social life of the many communities and neighbourhoods they serve. In their operation and in focusing on local needs, these centrally located community facilities offer ideal opportunities for diverse voluntary groups and organisations to engage in social interaction through a broad range of special interest activities and pursuits, events and programmes. Use of these facilities varies greatly and special efforts should be made to ensure that they are accessible by young people to cater for their needs.

Actions to support the achievement of Objective 6

Developing and funding recreation
- At central government level, appropriate interdepartmental/interagency groups should be established where key decisions are taken affecting the provision of facilities and programmes. Such groups should be informed by information/representation at local government level to ensure that gaps in service provision and the needs of the area are taken into account.
- Each City and County Development Board should lead on the preparation of an interagency recreation strategy for young people in their area. This should be advanced by the multi-agency Children's Services Committee (as provided for in *Towards 2016*) where this committee is in place.

- Local authorities, under the City and County Development Board process, will facilitate a network of Sports Officers, Arts Officers and representatives from Local Sports Partnerships, as well as representatives from the youth work sector, to exchange information and best practice.
- The Office of the Minister for Children, through the National Play Resource Centre, will develop a resource pack for local communities (including young people) to enable them to assess the recreation needs of young people in their area and how to access existing provision.
- The Office of the Minister for Children will pursue the potential of corporate community involvement at a national level to expand recreational opportunities for young people.
- Government departments and agencies at local level (including local authorities) will consider the opportunities available to them under existing funding lines to provide recreation programmes and facilities for young people.
- The Office of the Minister for Children will work with relevant Government departments to examine their spending programmes with a view to the adoption of a more integrated strategic approach to meeting prioritised needs at a level consistent with the National Recreation Policy.

Better use of existing facilities
- The Department of Education and Science will continue to explore the scope of making existing school buildings available to the community outside of school hours. Mechanisms should be put in place to ensure that shared school and community facilities or new school campuses are made available to the community.
- The operators and managers of locally based community facilities should be encouraged to make their premises available for use by young people.

chapter ten

OBJECTIVE 7:

Improve information on, evaluation and monitoring of recreational provision for young people in Ireland

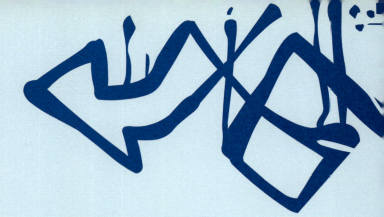

In the research commissioned by the Office of the Minister for Children to support the development of the National Recreation Policy, 'not knowing how to join' was cited by respondents as one of the main reasons for not joining in a range of popular activities (De Róiste and Dinneen, 2005). These included soccer (10%), dance (33%), rugby (22%), boxing (27%), swimming (19%), Gaelic football (18%), drama (27%) and youth clubs (33%). Another constraint that impacted on participation was young people's lack of knowledge about what was available in their localities and how to join activities. The latter view was reinforced by respondents in the public consultation, where a lack of information on recreation was mentioned as one of the barriers to participation in activities (OMC, 2006).

One of the top-ranking demands from Dáil na nÓg 2006 was the establishment of a national website with local links that would provide information to young people about facilities and activities for teenagers all over the country. Delegates at the Dáil said that young people found it difficult to get information on facilities and activities in their own locality and in other parts of the country. In response to this recommendation, the Minister for Children asked his Office (the Office of the Minister for Children) to set up a website to meet the needs of young people in this respect. A website company has been appointed to design the website and young people from the Coiste na dTeachtaí (the committee formed to follow up on the recommendations from Dáil na nÓg 2006) have been involved in its development and design. The Office of the Minister for Children has also approved funding for a webmaster, to develop information for the site and maintain it to meet the needs of young people. The Coiste na dTeachtaí will continue to be involved in the project, including in the development and content of the site. It is expected to launch the first phase of the website in Summer 2007.

In recognition that resources to support play are relatively underdeveloped in Ireland and that expertise in this area is comparatively limited, a provision was included in the National Play Policy for the establishment of a resource centre to provide information on play (NCO, 2004). The National Play Resource Centre has been operational since October 2005. As part of its role, the Centre will be responsible for the dissemination of information to young people on the range and location of recreation and leisure facilities at local level around the country on its website, www.playinireland.ie. Information will be provided about local authority facilities, such as swimming pools, libraries, multi-use games areas and skateboard parks. In addition, links will be provided to the website being developed by the Office of the Minister for Children (*see above*) and the websites of the following organisations:

- Vocational Education Committees (VECs), including information on the range of recreational facilities available for young people under work programmes at local level.
- National Youth Council of Ireland (NYCI), including links to the local VEC websites (*above*).
- Local authorities, Public Library Service and Local Sports Partnerships, including information at local level on the range of amenities and facilities available.
- Health Service Executive (HSE), including information on the facilities and programmes provided for young people nationally and with links to local HSE offices.

At local level, there is scope for management of local facilities to inform young people of events taking place through relatively simple means, such as putting up posters in local shops. This has been identified as an effective method of communication by young people themselves (Coiste na dTeachtaí). Local directories listing recreational facilities in the area can be a useful source of information (*see Box 36*).

Actions to support the achievement of Objective 7

- The Office of the Minister for Children, in consultation with Coiste na dTeachtaí, will develop a website to provide information to young people on facilities and activities in their localities.
- The National Play Resource Centre will disseminate information about facilities and activities for young people on its website.
- Vocational Education Committee websites should include information on the range of facilities that are available for young people under work programmes at local level. Links to these websites will be displayed by the National Youth Council of Ireland on its national website.
- Websites of local authorities, the Library Service and Local Sports Partnerships will provide information at local level on the range of amenities and facilities available.
- The Health Service Executive will provide information on the facilities and programmes provided for young people on its national website, with appropriate links to its local offices.

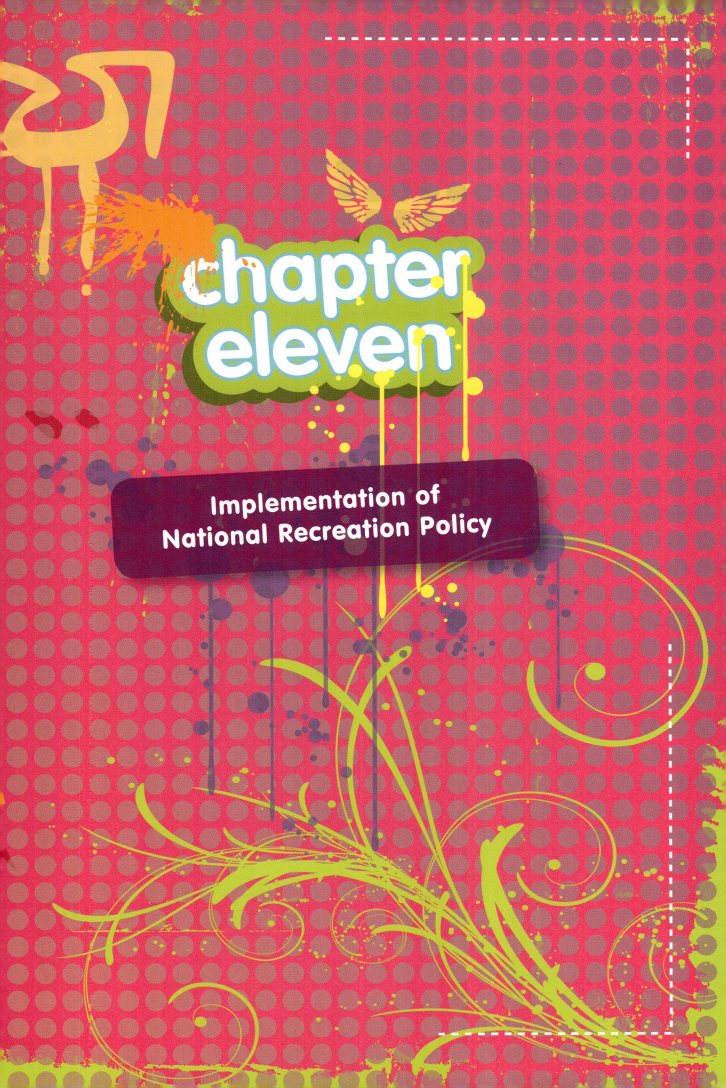

chapter eleven

Implementation of National Recreation Policy

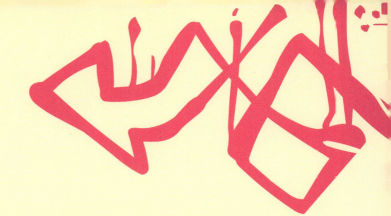

Review mechanisms

Individual Government departments, as key funding and delivery bodies at national and local level, will continue to retain responsibility for the implementation of measures that fall within the remit of their operational areas. In addition, while the programme of action largely concentrates on statutory provision, it is hoped that the private and commercial sectors will also draw on the policy when planning and developing new initiatives and outlets for young people.

A range of mechanisms will be put in place in order to review the roll-out, implementation and impact of the National Recreation Policy on young people (*see below*).

Monitoring at national level

A National Implementation Group — chaired by the Office of the Minister for Children and comprising representatives of key Government departments, the Health Service Executive, representatives of local authorities, the education sector and other key agencies as required — will drive forward and oversee the implementation of the National Recreation Policy and other policies for children and young people.

Cabinet Committee on Social Inclusion and Children

A review of progress on the implementation of the National Recreation Policy will be considered by the Cabinet Committee on Social Inclusion and Children, chaired by the Taoiseach and comprising relevant Government ministers, including the Minister for Children. The Cabinet Committee will monitor progress in implementing the National Recreation Policy and make recommendations as considered appropriate.

Local implementation

Improved recreational opportunities for young people at local level will be an important factor in determining the success of the National Recreation Policy. Each City and County Development Board will be required, on an annual basis, to review progress on the implementation of the policy at local level. This will be carried out in the context of the preparation of a local interagency recreation strategy by the Children's Committee within each City and County Development Board (which Committee is provided for in *Towards 2016*) that will involve the identification of key actions and priorities for implementation and delivery at local leve .

Performance indicators

The National Set of Child Well-being Indicators, developed by the Office of the Minister for Children under the National Children's Strategy (Hanafin and Brooks, 2005), will form a basis for measuring performance in achieving the objectives set out in the National Recreation Policy. The specific indicators identified include:

- The number of children aged 11, 13 and 15 who report to feel safe in the area where they l ve, expressed as a proportion of children in the same age groups.
- The number of children aged 11, 13 and 15 who report that there are good places in their area to spend their free time, expressed as a proportion of all children in the same age groups.
- The number of children aged 11, 13 and 15 who report to be physically active for (a) at least two hours and (b) more than four hours per week, expressed as a proportion of all children in the same age groups.

The resulting indicators will form part of the review of the implementation of the policy.

National Longitudinal Study of Children

The first phase of the National Longitudinal Study of Children in Ireland commenced in 2006. This study sets out to examine two nationally representative groups of children, one at 9 months old and the other at 9 years old. The nationally representative sample of 9-year-olds will include 8,000 children. The children will be interviewed at 9 years and at 13 years. The aim is to '*study the factors that contribute to or undermine the well-being of children in contemporary Irish families and, through this, contribute to the setting of effective and responsive policies relating to children and to the design of services for children and families*'.

An important component of this longitudinal study will be the extent to which children are involved in their communities and also the recreational opportunities afforded to them through their local community/ neighbourhood. This will provide important information for policy-makers and will enable developments over time to be evaluated.

Cost implications of the policy

As indicated in Chapter 1 and Appendix 1, there has been substantial investment in recreational programmes and facilities by a number of Government departments and agencies. However, one of the main gaps identified in the public consultation for this policy is the need for recreational opportunities for young people outside of competitive sport and, in particular, the requirement for more casual recreational opportunities, such as youth cafés and drop-in centres.

Other aspects of the policy, such as the further development of the youth work sector, will be addressed through the implementation of the Youth Work Development Plan.

The key aspects of the policy with cost implications are:
- provision of facilities;
- giving young people a voice in the design, implementation and monitoring of recreation policies and facilities;
- child-/youth-friendly environments;
- innovative arts work and physical activity programmes involving young people;
- targeted investment for young people with additional needs.

Provision of facilities

The key need identified in the public consultation for this policy was for youth cafés/drop-in centres. The costs of youth cafés can vary. The initial capital costs need not be high if there is a building available. The set-up costs (including refurbishment of an existing building and equipment costs) could be in the order of €120,000-€150,000. It is essential that provision be made for ongoing operational costs, including rent, staffing, electricity, telephone and security. The operational costs of the larger youth cafés (e.g. The Gaf in Galway and Squashy Couch in Waterford), including staffing costs, are approximately €300,000 per annum.

There is scope for providing youth cafes or drop-in centres at a variety of different levels. Apart from dedicated cafés, it is also recommended that existing facilities should include a space dedicated to young people where they can meet their friends in a safe environment. The cost associated with this would be substantially less, particularly if existing staff can be redeployed to work with the young people.

Multi-use games areas (MUGAs) cost in the order of €100,000-€150,000. There is scope for using Sports Capital funding to partially fund such facilities.

It is difficult to give an average cost for skateboard parks since it depends on the design. A number of skateboard parks under the current pilot project are estimated to cost €200,000-€300,000. Mobile skateboard facilities would be significantly less expensive.

Giving young people a voice in the design, implementation and monitoring of recreation policies and facilities

Consultation with and participation by young people is a key objective of this policy. The development of the Comhairle na nÓg structure to facilitate young people's participation at local level will be addressed by the Comhairle na nÓg Implementation Group. In the long term, consultation/participation will deliver improved value for money and will ensure that the provision of facilities and programmes will meet the needs of the young people who are using them.

Creation of child-/youth-friendly environments

The development of youth-friendly environments is central to this policy. This recognises that, in addition to facilities provided for them, young people's needs should also be met within the wider built and natural environment. This has resource implications, but these can be reduced if the requirements are built into the early stages of environmental design.

Innovative arts work with young people

This policy recommends the use of existing mechanisms for innovative projects involving young people, such as the Per Cent for Art Scheme. There is a need, however, for additional investment, particularly in relation to encouraging participation by young people in the arts and in enabling the National Cultural Institutions to engage more fully with teenagers. There is also a need for additional investment in summer-time activities, including summer festivals and innovative programmes engaging with young people during the summer holidays.

Physical activity

This policy recommends investment in Local Sports Partnerships in order to increase participation in physical activity (including youth dance) and address issues such as gender bias.

Targeted investment

This policy identifies groups of young people who are in need of more resource-intensive interventions. Specific investment could include the following:

- Programmes targeting young people in rural areas, e.g. additional investment in the Rural Transport Initiative specifically to provide services to young people, including Friday nights and at weekends.
- The Public Library Service to extend the library service to young people in rural areas.
- Investment in appropriate mobile facilities.
- Specific investment in activities that have a traditional appeal to young people who are disadvantaged or at risk (e.g. boxing).

- Through the Department of Education and Science, to provide additional financial assistance to recreation projects for young Travellers, particularly those that include girls.
- Provision and equipping of dedicated teenage recreational space in hospitals.
- Funding for bodies that work to integrate young people with disabilities and other young people in a recreational setting (e.g. Best Buddies Programme).
- Funding to help mainstream some of the Young Social Innovators projects.

Strategic direction

This policy is not just about additional expenditure. It also aims to provide strategic direction to Government departments, local authorities, City and County Development Boards, the youth sector, the community and voluntary sectors, and other interested parties to develop recreational opportunities for young people in an informed and appropriate manner within existing funding lines.

Implementation Action Plan

Each of the seven objectives in the National Recreation Policy incorporates a series of corresponding actions for priority implementation by various Government departments and agencies. These will have a crucial role to play in their delivery within the overall framework of the policy. Full details of the Implementation Action Plan are set out in the following pages, with the appropriate actions proposed under each objective and assigning responsibilities and timescales for achieving those actions.

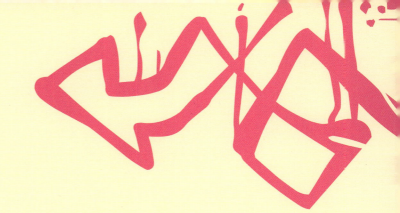

OBJECTIVE 1: Give young people a voice in the design, implementation and monitoring of recreation policies and facilities

No.	Action	Responsibility	Target date
1	A condition of funding for projects/programmes arising as a result of the National Recreation Policy will be that young people will be consulted and actively involved in the design, planning and, where appropriate, management of facilities and programmes. Young people will also be involved in the post-evaluation of recreation programmes.	Funding/Lead department	2007 and ongoing
2	Consultations undertaken in relation to the provision of recreational facilities will include young people. This would include facilities where they are one of the user groups, as well as where the facility is designed specifically for them.	Funding/Lead department	2007 and ongoing
3	Guidelines and criteria for the active participation of young people in all aspects of youth work provision (including governance) will be developed as recommended under the National Youth Work Development Plan. These will be phased in as part of the requirements for statutory funding of youth work organisations and initiatives.	Department of Education and Science	2008
4	While recognising that the Youth Work Act 2001 provides for the inclusion of young people under the age of 25 on Voluntary Youth Councils, special efforts will be made to include young people under 18, where practicable, on the councils.	Department of Education and Science	2008
5	The Office of the Minister for Children will advise public bodies and monitor the implementation of the participation guidelines, *Young Voices*.	Office of the Minister for Children	2007 and ongoing
6	Arising from the review of the Comhairle na nÓg structure, the Comhairle na nÓg Implementation Group, established by the Office of the Minister for Children, will make recommendations to ensure the development of effective Comhairle na nÓg under each City and County Development Board.	Office of the Minister for Children	2007
7	Local authorities will utilise the Comhairle na nÓg structure to inform relevant City and County Strategies/Plans, particularly in relation to recreational facilities and community and amenity programmes.	Local authorities	2007 and ongoing
8	Local authorities will encourage young people to participate on relevant sub-committees and through the Community and Voluntary Forums to avail of opportunities to become members of Strategic Policy Committees, particularly those addressing community, recreation and amenity issues.	Local authorities	2007 and ongoing

Objective 1 *(continued)*

9	Local authorities will maximise the use of existing mecha-nisms to provide for young people's involvement in Estate Management Committees.	Local authorities	2007 and ongoing

OBJECTIVE 2: Promote organised activities for young people and examine ways to motivate them to be involved

No.	Action	Responsibility	Target date
10	Further resources will be provided to progress implementation of the National Youth Work Development Plan 2003-2007 and the Youth Work Act 2001 on a phased and prioritised basis.	Department of Education and Science	2007 – 2009
11	Management authorities of second-level schools will be encouraged to include youth volunteering in their Transition Year programmes.	Department of Education and Science	2007 and ongoing
12	The Task Force on Active Citizenship will advise on measures to promote voluntary activity among young people and on mechanisms for maintaining and increasing the numbers of adult volunteers.	Task Force on Active Citizenship	2007
13	The Arts Council will promote a local partnership approach with local authorities, the youth work sector and other relevant agencies to further develop arts provision and opportunities for young people.	Arts Council Local authorities	2007 and ongoing
14	Local authorities will examine the feasibility of using funding available to upgrade existing facilities to provide band practice rooms for young people. The Office of the Minister for Children will also raise with the Department of Community, Rural and Gaeltacht Affairs the feasibility of using Dormant Accounts funding for this purpose.	Local authorities Office of the Minister for Children Department of Community, Rural and Gaeltacht Affairs	2007 and ongoing
15	Public authorities engaged in large-scale public infrastructural projects will be advised that a proportion of the Per Cent for Art Scheme should be allocated specifically to innovative projects involving young people.	Department of Arts, Sport and Tourism	2007

Objective 2 _(continued)_

16	The Department of Arts, Sport and Tourism, in conjunction with the National Cultural Institutions, will undertake research on how best to improve young people's access to the cultural institutions.	Department of Arts, Sport and Tourism National Cultural Institutions	2007
17	Local authorities, through Comhairle na nÓg, will involve young people in local authority arts and cultural provision.	Local authorities	2007 and ongoing
18	The Arts Council, through Local Arts Officers, will work with the Irish Sports Council through Local Sports Partnerships and VEC-funded Sports Committees to provide improved opportunities for youth dance.	Arts Council Irish Sports Council	2007 and ongoing
19	Local Sports Partnerships will develop programmes to increase participation in physical activity, promote lifelong involvement and address key issues such as gender bias.	Irish Sports Council Local Sports Partnerships	2007 and ongoing
20	The Irish Sports Council will include in its Strategy on Lifelong Involvement a greater emphasis on recreational sport and non-traditional activities in order to promote physical activity.	Irish Sports Council	2007

OBJECTIVE 3: Ensure that the recreational needs of young people are met through the development of youth-friendly and safe environments

No.	Action	Responsibility	Target date
21	Existing facilities should include a space dedicated to young people where they can meet their friends in a safe environment. A dedicated space should also be included as part of the design of new community facilities, including libraries, and facilities funded under the Young People's Facilities and Services Fund. Health and other relevant information, as well as education on a range of relevant topics, should be available to young people in these settings.	Local authorities Libraries Department of Community, Rural and Gaeltacht Affairs Department of Social and Family Affairs	2007 and ongoing
22	Resources permitting and following a local needs assessment, dedicated youth cafés should be provided on a phased basis, particularly in areas where there are high concentrations of young people between the ages of 12-18. These youth cafés/drop-in centres should be introduced in consultation with young people.	Lead department	2007 and ongoing
23	A formal partnership should be entered into with other relevant State agencies to provide health and other relevant services/information in these settings.	Department of Social and Family Affairs (through the Family Support Agency) Department of Education and Science Health Service Executive	2007 and ongoing
24	An Chomhairle Leabharlanna, in association with the library authorities and the Office of the Minister for Children, will investigate ways in which to develop services in public libraries in partnership with young people.	An Chomhairle Leabharlanna Office of the Minister for Children	2007
25	There should be appropriate community involvement, including the use of mechanisms such as 'Planning for Real', in the provision of outdoor facilities for young people.	Local authorities	2007 and ongoing

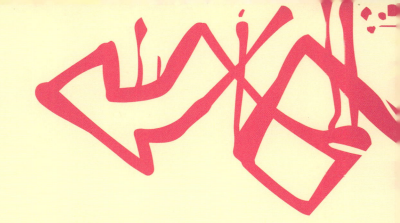

26	Joint Policing Committees will consider the participation of young people in local policing forums, when established.	Department of Justice, Equality and Law Reform Garda Síochána	2007 and ongoing
27	Young people will be active participants in regeneration projects, particularly in the design, use and care of public spaces.	Local authorities	2007 and ongoing
28	The Office of the Minister for Children will work with Dublin City Council and other relevant agencies to develop a youth-proofing model to facilitate local authorities in ensuring that young people are involved in their plans, policies and programmes.	Office of the Minister for Children Dublin City Council	2007
29	Adopting a 'Home Zone' approach will be examined in planning new developments.	Local authorities	2007 and ongoing
30	The Residential Density Guidelines, to be introduced by the Department of the Environment, Heritage and Local Government, will refer specifically to the need to identify at an early stage the preferred location of quality open spaces, as well as other recreational facilities, and provide for more casual spaces suitable for smaller children's play.	Department of the Environment, Heritage and Local Government	2007
31	Local authorities and RAPID will consider the provision of additional multi-use games areas.	Local authorities Department of Community, Rural and Gaeltacht Affairs	2007 and ongoing
32	Joint Policing Committees, to be established under the Garda Síochána Act 2005, will examine the potential for the provision of youth shelters.	Department of Justice, Equality and Law Reform	2007 and ongoing
33	Local authorities will review the operation of the pilot skateboard park scheme, introduced by the Department of the Environment, Heritage and Local Government, with a view to identifying potential opportunities for the provision of more facilities based on the recreational needs of young people in their areas.	Local authorities	2007 and ongoing

OBJECTIVE 4: Maximise the range of recreational opportunities available for young people who are marginalised, disadvantaged or who have a disability

No.	Action	Responsibility	Target date
34	The National Spatial Strategy, the National Rural Development Programme and expenditure under the National Development Plan will have regard to the provision of social and community infrastructure, such as parks, sporting and cultural facilities, that will meet the needs of young people.	Lead departments	2007 and ongoing
35	The development of the Sports Facilities Strategy should take account of key issues affecting young people in rural areas and their ability to access facilities.	Department of Arts, Sport and Tourism	2007 and ongoing
36	The mainstreamed Rural Transport Initiative should specifically address the needs of young people in rural areas to access recreational facilities locally.	Department of Transport	2007 and ongoing
37	The Department of the Environment, Heritage and Local Government, through the local authorities and the Department of Community, Rural and Gaeltacht Affairs, will examine the feasibility of providing more mobile facilities in rural areas.	Department of the Environment, Heritage and Local Government Local authorities Department of Community, Rural and Gaeltacht Affairs	2007 and ongoing
38	The Department of the Environment, Heritage and Local Government, through the Public Library Service, will examine the feasibility of expanding rural library initiatives for young people in rural areas.	Department of the Environment, Heritage and Local Government An Chomhairle Leabharlanna	2007 and ongoing
39	Local development programmes such as RAPID and CLÁR, as well as Measure C of the Local Development Social Inclusion Programme and LEADER, will identify the potential for actively supporting improved recreation provision for young people within disadvantaged communities, including activities during the summer holidays (in circumstances where they are not already being provided by the local authorities).	Department of Community, Rural and Gaeltacht Affairs	2007 and ongoing

Objective 4 *(continued)*

40	Young people at risk should be consulted and actively involved in projects and programmes designed for them.	Department of Education and Science Department of Community, Rural and Gaeltacht Affairs Garda Síochána	2007 and ongoing
41	Further research to be carried out on how to motivate young people at risk to engage in positive leisure activities.	Department of Education and Science Office of the Minister for Children	2007 – 2008
42	The Office of the Minister for Children will raise with the Department of Community, Rural and Gaeltacht Affairs the feasibility of using Dormant Accounts funding to provide support for activities that have a traditional appeal to youth in disadvantaged areas or at risk.	Office of the Minister for Children Department of Community, Rural and Gaeltacht Affairs	2007 and ongoing
43	The Garda Juvenile Diversion Programme will be expanded to 100 projects in 2007.	Garda Síochána	2007
44	Boards of Management should be encouraged to make teenagers from ethnic minorities aware of after-school activities and facilitate young people to participate in them.	Department of Education and Science	2007
45	The Libraries and Cultural Diversity Project Team will make recommendations on the development of library services for the multicultural society in Ireland.	An Chomhairle Leabharlanna	2007
46	The National Consultative Council on Racism and Interculturalism will look specifically at the needs of young people from ethnic minority groups and how these can best be met by existing providers.	National Consultative Council on Racism and Interculturalism	2007 and ongoing
47	The National Youth Council of Ireland, with the support of the Department of Education and Science, will take the lead in the development of an Intercultural Strategy for the youth work sector.	National Youth Council of Ireland Department of Education and Science	2007 and ongoing

Objective 4 *(continued)*

48	Further research should be undertaken with young Travellers to determine the extent of discrimination against them when they attempt to engage in mainstream recreation. Issues emerging from the research will be addressed in the National Action Plan against Racism.	Department of Justice, Equality and Law Reform National Consultative Council on Racism and Interculturalism	2007
49	The Department of Education and Science, through the youth work sector, will continue to provide financial assistance to recreational and development projects for young Travellers, including girls.	Department of Education and Science	2007 and ongoing
50	The Office of the Minister for Children will include young Travellers in its Children and Young People's Forum, established to advise the Minister on the implementation of the National Children's Strategy.	Office of the Minister for Children	2007
51	Hospitals in which adolescent patients are treated will work towards providing an environment that is suitable and adaptable to their recreational needs.	Health Service Executive	2007 and ongoing
52	The implementation of Article 7 of the Charter for Children in Hospital will be specifically addressed in the development of the new Children's Hospital (Department of Health and Children/HSE) and in its ultimate operation (HSE).	Department of Health and Children Health Service Executive	2007 and ongoing
53	City and County Development Boards should pay particular attention to recruiting young people with disabilities to Comhairle na nÓg.	City and County Development Boards	2007 and ongoing
54	Strategies developed for young people's recreation locally should specifically address issues relating to the involvement of young people with disabilities in mainstream recreation.	Office of the Minister for Children National Youth Council of Ireland	2007
55	Sectoral plans will be implemented by the relevant Government departments to implement Part 3 of the Disability Act 2005, dealing with access to buildings and services.	Relevant Government departments	2007 and ongoing
56	The Department of Education and Science should highlight the value of projects such as "Sport for All" in ensuring that PE programmes in schools are planned and implemented to include students with disabilities	Department of Education and Science	2007 and ongoing

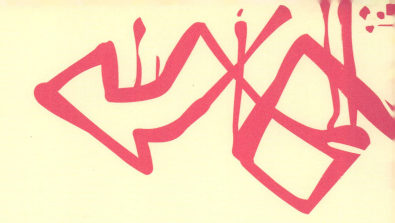

OBJECTIVE 5: Promote relevant qualifications/standards in the provision of recreational activities

No.	Action	Responsibility	Target date
57	The Health Service Executive will provide a web page on its website designed for young people, parents and the community and voluntary sectors with information on child protection and the requirements of the *Children First* guidelines. A link to this will be provided by the Office of the Minister for Children and the National Play Resource Centre.	Health Service Executive Office of the Minister for Children National Play Resource Centre	2007
58	The obstacles to the vetting of people having substantial, unsupervised access to young people in recreational settings will be removed by the ongoing phased implementation of the Report of the Working Group on Garda Vetting.	Department of Justice, Equality and Law Reform	2007 and ongoing
59	The Minister for Justice, Equality and Law Reform will continue to explore proposals for legislation to regularise criminal history vetting.	Department of Justice, Equality and Law Reform	2007/2008
60	The Department of Transport will put in place the Adventure Activities Standards Authority, or assign the functions to another appropriate body, to regulate adventure activities.	Department of Transport	2007
61	Related to the issue of drop-out from activities, publicly funded organisations working with young people in the youth work sector, the sports sector and the arts sector will continue to make arrangements to ensure that both staff and volunteers receive appropriate training in working with young people in recreational settings.	Department of Education and Science Department of Arts, Sport and Tourism	2007 and ongoing
62	Youth organisations will be encouraged to ensure that contracts for staff working with young people reflect any out-of-hours requirements of the job.	Office of the Minister for Children	2007

OBJECTIVE 6: Develop a partnership approach in developing and funding recreational opportunities across the statutory, community and voluntary sectors

No.	Action	Responsibility	Target date
63	At central government level, appropriate interdepartmental/interagency groups should be established where key decisions are taken affecting the provision of facilities and programmes. Such groups should be informed by information/representation at local government level to ensure that gaps in service provision and the needs of the area are taken into account.	Department of Arts, Sport and Tourism Department of Community, Rural and Gaeltacht Affairs Local authorities Vocational Education Committees	2007 and ongoing
64	Each City and County Development Board should lead on the preparation of an interagency recreation strategy for young people in their area. This should be advanced by the multi-agency Children's Services Committee (as provided for in Towards 2016) where this committee is in place.	City and County Development Boards Relevant agencies	2008 and ongoing
65	Local authorities, under the City and County Development Board process, will facilitate a network of Sports Officers, Arts Officers and representatives from Local Sports Partnerships, as well as representatives from the youth work sector, to exchange information and best practice.	Local authorities	2007 and ongoing
66	The Office of the Minister for Children, through the National Play Resource Centre, will develop a resource pack for local communities (including young people) to enable them to assess the recreational needs of young people in their area and how to access existing provision.	Office of the Minister for Children National Play Resource Centre	2008
67	The Office of the Minister for Children will pursue the potential of corporate community involvement at a national level to expand recreational opportunities for young people.	Office of the Minister for Children Corporate sector	2008 and ongoing
68	Government departments and agencies at local level (including local authorities) will consider the opportunities available to them under existing funding lines to provide recreation programmes and facilities for young people.	Government departments Agencies Local authorities	2007 and ongoing

Objective 6 *(continued)*

69	The Office of the Minister for Children will work with relevant Government departments to examine their spending programmes with a view to the adoption of a more integrated strategic approach to meeting prioritised needs at a level consistent with the National Recreation Policy.	Office of the Minister for Children Departments of Arts, Sport and Tourism; Environment, Heritage and Local Government; Community, Rural and Gaeltacht Affairs; and Education and Science	2007 and ongoing
70	The Department of Education and Science will continue to explore the scope of making existing school buildings available to the community outside of school hours. Mechanisms should be put in place to ensure that shared school and community facilities or new school campuses are made available to the community.	Department of Education and Science	2007 and ongoing
71	The operators and managers of locally based community facilities should be encouraged to make their premises available for use by young people.	Relevant Government departments and agencies	2007 and ongoing

OBJECTIVE 7: Improve information on, evaluation and monitoring of recreational provision for young people in Ireland

No.	Action	Responsibility	Target date
72	The Office of the Minister for Children, in consultation with Coiste na dTeachtaí, will develop a website to provide information to young people on facilities and activities in their localities.	Office of the Minister for Children Coiste na dTeachtaí	2007 and ongoing
73	The National Play Resource Centre will also disseminate information about facilities and activities for young people on its website.	National Play Resource Centre	2007 and ongoing
74	Vocational Education Committee websites should include information on the range of facilities that are available for young people under work programmes at local level. Links to these websites will be displayed by the National Youth Council of Ireland on its national website.	Vocational Education Committees National Youth Council of Ireland	2007 and ongoing
75	Websites of local authorities, the Library Service and Local Sports Partnerships will provide information at local level on the range of amenities and facilities available.	Local authorities Library Service Local Sports Partnerships	2007 and ongoing
76	The Health Service Executive will provide information on the facilities and programmes provided for young people on its national website, with appropriate links to its local offices.	Health Service Executive	2007 and ongoing

Alderson, P. (1993) 'European charter of children's rights', *Bulletin of Medical Ethics*, October 1993, pp. 13-15.

Arts Council (2005) *Partnership for the Arts: Arts Council Goals 2006-2010*. Dublin: The Arts Council.

Arts Council (2006) *Guidelines for the Protection and Welfare of Children and Young People in the Arts Sector*. Dublin: The Arts Council.

Ballymun Partnership (2005) *Ballymun Partnership Magazine Summer 2005*. Dublin: Ballymun Partnership.

Ballymun Regeneration Ltd (1998) *Ballymun Regeneration Masterplan*. Dublin: Ballymun Regeneration Ltd.

BCI (2004) *Children's Advertising Code*. Dublin: Broadcasting Commission of Ireland.

Boreham, C. and Riddoch, C. (2001) 'The physical activity, fitness and health of children', *Journal of Sports Science*, Vol. 19, No. 1, pp. 915-29.

Borland, M., Hill, M., Laybourn, A. and Stafford, A. (2001) *Improving consultation with children and young people in relevant aspects of policy-making and legislation in Scotland*. Edinburgh: The Scottish Parliament.

Byrne, T., Nixon, E., Mayock, P. and Whyte, J. (2006) *Free time and leisure needs of young people living in marginalised communities*. Dublin: Combat Poverty Agency.

Calfas, K.J., Sallis, J.F., Lovato, C.Y. and Campbell, J. (1994) 'Physical activity and its determinants before and after college graduation', *Medicine, Exercise, Nutrition and Health*, No. 3, pp. 323-34.

Centre for Health Promotion Studies (2003) *National Health and Lifestyle Surveys*. Galway: Centre for Health Promotion Studies, National University of Ireland.

Chawla, J.C. (1994) 'Sport for people with disability', *British Medical Journal*, No. 308, pp. 1500-04.

Child Accident Prevention Trust (2002) *Taking Chances: The lifestyles and leisure risk of young people*. London: Child Accident Prevention Trust.

Children in Hospital Ireland (1995) *Guidelines for the Care of Adolescents in Hospital*. Dublin: Children in Hospital Ireland.

Chomhairle Leabharlanna (2005a) *Irish Library News, No. 249, April 2005*. Dublin: Irish Library Council.

Chomhairle Leabharlanna (2005b) *Irish Library News, No. 251, June 2005*. Dublin: Irish Library Council.

Cleary, A. and Prizeman, G. (1999) *Homelessness and Mental Health*. Dublin: Combat Poverty Agency/ Homelessness and Mental Health Action Group.

Cohn, E. (2000) 'Market Watch', *American Prospect*, Vol. 11, No. 6. Available at www.prospect.org

Commissioner for Children and Young People, Scotland's (2006) *Safe, Active, Happy: Action Plan 2006-2008*. Edinburgh: Scotland's Commissioner for Children and Young People.

Connolly, J.F. and Lester, D. (2000) 'Suicide rates in Irish counties', *Irish Journal of Psychological Medicine*, Vol. 17, No. 2, pp. 59-61.

Connor, S. (2003) *Youth Sport in Ireland: The sporting, leisure and lifestyle patterns of Irish adolescents*. Dublin: The Liffey Press.

Cork Association for the Deaf (2005) Personal correspondence, quoted in De Róiste and Dinneen (2005).

Council of National Cultural Institutions (2004) *A Policy Framework for Education, Community, Outreach*. Dublin: Council of Cultural Institutions.

Coughlan, M. (2002) *The Participation of Young People in the Arts in Ireland. A proposal policy and action plan for the period of the Third Arts Plan*. Dublin: The Arts Council.

Cowling, J. (ed.) (2004) *For Arts Sake? Society and the Arts in the 21st century*. London: Institute for Public Policy Research. Quoted in the Arts Council's submission to *The Report of the Public Consultation for the Development of the National Recreation Policy for Young People*.

Coyne, I., Gallagher, P. and Regan, G. (2006) *Giving children a voice: Investigation of children's experiences of participation in consultation and decision-making within the Irish healthcare setting*, Office of the Minister for Children. Dublin: The Stationery Office.

Crawford, D., Jackson, E. and Godbey, G. (1991) 'A hierarchical model of leisure constraints', *Leisure Sciences*, No. 13, pp. 309-20.

Crime Council (2003) *A Crime Prevention Strategy for Ireland tackling the concerns of local communities.* Dublin: The Stationery Office.

Cronin, J. (2001) *Irish Youth Theatre Handbook: A guide to good practice in youth drama.* Dublin: National Association of Youth Drama.

CSO (unpublished) *Usual residents by country, age group, sex and nationality, Census 2002.*

CSO (2003) *Census 2002: Principal Demographic Results.* Cork: Central Statistics Office.

CSO (2004a) *Quarterly National Household Survey: Educational Attainment, 1999 to 2003.* Cork: Central Statistics Office.

CSO (2004b) *2002 Census. Volume 8: Irish Traveller Community.* Cork: Central Statistics Office.

CSO (2006) *Quarterly National Household Survey: Educational Attainment, 2002 to 2005.* Cork: Central Statistics Office.

Department of Education and Science (2003a) *National Youth Work Development Plan 2003-2007.* Dublin: The Stationery Office.

Department of Education and Science (2003b) *Code of Good Practice — Child Protection for the Youth Work Sector*, 2nd Edition. Dublin: The Stationery Office.

Department of Education and Science (2004) *Rules and Programme for Secondary Schools 2004/05.* Dublin: The Stationery Office.

Department of Education and Skills (UK) (2003) *The UK Programme 'Positive Activities for Young People'* (press release, 15 July 2003). London: HMSO.

Department of the Environment and Local Government (1998) *Branching Out: A New Public Library Service.* Dublin: The Stationery Office.

Department of the Environment and Local Government (1999) *Planning Guidelines on Residential Density.* Dublin: The Stationery Office.

Department of the Environment, Heritage and Local Government (2002) *National Spatial Strategy for Ireland 2002-2020. People, Places, Potential.* Dublin: The Stationery Office.

Department of the Environment, Heritage and Local Government (2005) *Housing Policy Framework: Building Sustainable Communities.* Dublin: The Stationery Office.

Department of Health and Children (1999) *Children First: National Guidelines for the Protection and Welfare of Children.* Dublin: The Stationery Office.

Department of Health and Children (2000a) *National Children's Strategy: Our Children — Their Lives.* Dublin: The Stationery Office.

Department of Health and Children (2000b) *Report of the Public Consultation for the National Children's Strategy.* Dublin: The Stationery Office.

Department of Health and Children (2000c) *National Health Promotion Strategy 2000-2005.* Dublin: The Stationery Office.

Department of Health and Children (2002) *Our Duty to Care: The principles of good practice for the protection of children and young people.* Dublin: The Stationery Office.

Department of Health and Children (2004) *Strategic Task Force on Alcohol. Second Report, September 2004*, Health Promotion Unit. Dublin: The Stationery Office.

Department of Health and Children (2005) *Report of the National Task Force on Obesity, 2005.* Dublin: The Stationery Office.

Department of Justice (1995) *Report of the Task Force on the Travelling Community.* Dublin: The Stationery Office.

Department of Justice, Equality and Law Reform (2004) *Report of Working Group on Garda Vetting.* Dublin: Department of Justice, Equality and Law Reform.

Department of Justice, Equality and Law Reform (2005a) *Planning for Diversity: National Action Plan against Racism.* Dublin: The Stationery Office.

Department of Justice, Equality and Law Reform (2005b) *Report on the Youth Justice Review*. Dublin: The Stationery Office.

Department of Justice, Equality and Law Reform (2006) *Report of the High Level Group on Traveller Issues*. Dublin: The Stationery Office.

Department of the Taoiseach (2006) *Towards 2016: Ten-Year Framework Social Partnership Agreement 2006-2015*. Dublin: The Stationery Office.

Department of Transport (2005) *Transport 21*. Dublin: The Stationery Office.

Department of Transport, Local Government and the Regions (UK) (1997) *Youth and Regeneration: Good Practice Guide*. London: HMSO.

Department of Transport, Local Government and the Regions (UK) (2002) *Green Spaces, Better Spaces*. London: Urban Green Spaces Task Force.

Department of Urban Affairs and Planning (Australia) (1999) *Urban Design Guidelines*. Sydney: Urban Design Advisory Service.

De Róiste, A. and Dinneen, J. (2005) *Young People's Views about Opportunities, Barriers and Supports to Recreation and Leisure*, Cork Institute of Technology and National Children's Office. Dublin: The Stationery Office.

Devlin, M. (2006) *Inequality and the stereotyping of young people*. Dublin: Equality Authority.

Donegal County Council (2005) *Taobh Tíre: A Better Library Service for Rural Areas*. Donegal: Donegal County Council.

Dowda, M., Pate, R.R., Felton, G.M., Saunders, R., Ward, D.S., Dishman, R.K. and Trost, S.G. (2004) 'Physical activities and sedentary pursuits in African American and Caucasian girls', *Research Quarterly for Exercise and Sport*, Vol. 75, No. 4, pp. 352-61.

Driver, B.L. (1992) 'The Benefits of Leisure', *Parks and Recreation*, No. 27, pp. 16-23.

Dublin City Council (2004) *Operational Standards for Dublin City Council-run Youth, Community and Sport Centres*. Dublin: Dublin City Council.

Dworkin, J., Larson, R. and Hansen, D. (2003) 'Adolescents' accounts of growth experiences in youth activities', *Journal of Youth and Adolescence*, Vol. 32, No. 1, pp.17-27.

Edwards, L. and Hatch, B. (2003) *Passing Time: A report about young people and communities*. London: Institute for Public Policy Research.

Elsey, S. (2004) 'Children's Experience of Public Space', *Children and Society*, Vol. 18, No. 2, pp. 155-64 (Special Issue, April 2004: 'Children, Young People and Participation').

ESPAD (2003) *The European School Survey Project on Alcohol and Other Drugs, Report 2003*. Stockholm: Swedish Council for Information on Alcohol and Other Drugs (CAN) and the Pompidou Group at the Council of Europe.

Eurostat (2005) *Europe in figures: Eurostat Yearbook 2005*. Brussels: Eurostat.

Fahey, T., Delaney, L. and Gannon, B. (2005) *School children and sport in Ireland*. Dublin: Economic and Social Research Institute.

Fahey, T., Layte, R. and Gannon, B. (2004) *Sport participation and health among adults in Ireland*. Dublin: Economic and Social Research Institute.

FGS Consulting and Children's Research Centre, TCD (2006) *Research on Youth Volunteering*. Dublin: National Children's Advisory Council.

Government of Ireland (1999a) *Irish Sports Council Act, 1999*. Dublin: The Stationery Office.

Government of Ireland (1999b) *Qualifications (Education and Training) Act, 1999*. Dublin: The Stationery Office.

Government of Ireland (2000) *Equal Status Act 2000*. Dublin: The Stationery Office.

Government of Ireland (2001a) *Adventure Activities Standards Authority Act 2001*. Dublin: The Stationery Office.

Government of Ireland (2001b) *Local Government Act 2000*. Dublin: The Stationery Office.

Government of Ireland (2001c) *Youth Work Act 2001*. Dublin: The Stationery Office.

Government of Ireland (2002) *An Agreed Programme for Government between Fianna Fáil and the Progressive Democrats.* Dublin: The Stationery Office.

Government of Ireland (2004) *Equal Status Act 2004.* Dublin: The Stationery Office.

Government of Ireland (2005) *Garda Síochána Act 2005.* Dublin: The Stationery Office.

Grotevant, H.D., Thornbecke W.L. and Meyer M.L. (1982) 'An extension of Marcia's Identity Status Interview into the interpersonal domain', *Journal of Youth and Adolescence*, Vol. 11, No. 1, pp. 33-47.

Hamburg, D.A. and Takanishi, R. (1989) 'Preparing for life: The critical transition of adolescence', *American Psychologist*, Vol. 44, No. 5, pp. 825-27.

Hanafin, S. and Brooks, A.M. (2005) *Report on the development of a National Set of Child Well-being Indicators*, National Children's Office. Dublin: The Stationery Office.

Hanna, J.L. (1988) *Dance and Stress: Resistance, reduction and euphoria*. New York: AMS Press Inc.

Hansen, C.H. and Hansen, R.D. (1990) 'Rock Music Videos and Antisocial Behavior', *Basic Applied Social Psychology,* Vol. 11, No. 4, pp. 357-69.

Harland, J. and Kinder, K. (eds.) (1999) *Crossing the Line: Extending young people's access to cultural venues*. London: Calouste Gulbenkian Foundation.

Health Promotion Research Centre (2003) *National Health and Life Style Surveys,* Department of Health and Children. Dublin: The Stationery Office.

Health Research Board (2003) *Annual Report and Accounts 2001*. Dublin: Health Research Board.

Health Research Board (2004) *Annual Report and Accounts 2002*. Dublin: Health Research Board.

Hendry, L.B., Schucksmith, J., Love, J. and Glendinning, A. (1993) *Young People's Leisure and Lifestyles*. London: Routledge.

Heywood, P., Crane, P., Egginton, A. and Gleeson, J. (1998) *Out and About: In or Out? Better outcomes from young people's use of public and community space in the city of Brisbane. Volume 2: Policies, implementation strategies and tools.* Brisbane: Brisbane City Council, Community Development Team West.

HSE (2005) *Reach Out: National Strategy for Action on Suicide Prevention 2005-2014*. Dublin: Health Service Executive.

Ingledew. D.K. and Sullivan, G. (2002) 'Effects of body mass and body image on exercise motives in adolescence', *Psychology of Sport and Exercise*, Vol. 3, No. 4, pp. 323-38.

Internet Advisory Board (2005) *Get with IT! A parents' guide to new media: Understanding and sharing the new media technologies with your children.* Dublin: Internet Advisory Board.

Irish Cellular Industry Association (2005) *A Parents' Guide to Mobile Phones*. Dublin: Irish Cellular Industry Association.

Irish Cellular Industry Association (2006) *Code of Practice for the responsible and secure use of mobile services*. Dublin: Irish Cellular Industry Association.

Irish Sports Council (2003) *Sport for life: The Irish Sports Council Statement of Strategy 2003-2005*. Dublin: Irish Sports Council.

Irish Sports Council (2005) *The Irish Sports Council's Challenge Funding Project 2005*. Dublin: Irish Sports Council.

Irish Sports Council and Sports Council for Northern Ireland (2006) *Code of Ethics in Sport for Children and Young People*. Dublin: Irish Sports Council.

Kirby, P., Lanyon, C., Cronin, K. and Sinclair, R. (2003) *Building a Culture of Participation — Involving young people in policy, service planning, delivery and evaluation*. London: Department for Education and Skills.

Laidlaw Foundation (2001) *Literature review on learning through recreation*. Canada: Family Network of Canadian Policy Research Networks.

Larson, R.W. (1995) 'Secrets in the bedroom: Adolescents' private use of media', *Journal of Youth and Adolescence*, Vol. 24, No. 5, pp. 535-50.

Larson, R.W. and Kubey, R. (1983) 'Television and music: Contrasting media in adolescent's life', *Youth and Society*, Vol. 15, No. 1, pp. 13-31.

Larson, R.W. and Verma, S. (1999) 'How children and adolescents spend time around the world: Work, play and developmental opportunities', *Psychological Bulletin*, No. 125, pp. 701-36.

Lewko, J.H. and Greendorfer, S.L. (1988) 'Family influences in sport socialisation of children and adolescents', in *Children in sport*, 3rd Edition, F.L. Smoll, R.A. Magill and M.A. Ash (eds.). Champaign, IL: Human Kinetics Publishers.

Local Government Focus (2000) *Australia's National Local Government Newspaper online*. Thornbury: Eryl Morgan Publications Pty Ltd.

Mahoney, J.L. and Cairns, R.B. (1997) 'Do school extracurricular activities protect against early school drop-out?', *Development Psychology*, No. 33, pp. 241-53.

McCoy, S. and Smyth, E. (2004) *At work in school: Part-time employment among second-level students*. Dublin: Economic and Social Research Institute/Liffey Press.

McCrea, N. (2003) *Steps towards inclusion: Developing youth work with separated children*. Dublin: Youth Action against Racism and Discrimination.

McGee, R., Williams, S., Howden-Chapman, P., Martin, J. and Kawachi, I. (2006) 'Participation in clubs and groups from childhood to adolescence and its effects on attachment and self-esteem', *Journal of Adolescence*, Vol. 29, No. 1, pp. 1-17.

Mainprize, S. (1985) 'Interpreting adolescents' music', *Journal of Child Care*, No. 2, pp. 55-62.

Matthews, H. (2001) *Children and Community Regeneration*. London: Save the Children.

National Children's Advisory Council (2002) *Advice to the Minister on the implementation of Children First and Vetting*. Dublin: National Children's Advisory Council.

National Children's Advisory Council (2006) *Research on Youth Volunteering in Ireland*. Available at www.ncac.ie

National Committee on Volunteering (2002) *Tipping the balance: Report of the National Committee on Volunteering*. Dublin: National Committee on Volunteering.

NCO (2004) *Ready, Steady, Play! A National Play Policy*, National Children's Office. Dublin: The Stationery Office.

NCO (2005a) *A Consultation Document for a Recreation Policy for Young People in Ireland*, National Children's Office. Dublin: The Stationery Office.

NCO (2005b) *Dáil na nÓg Delegates Report 2005*, National Children's Office. Dublin: The Stationery Office.

NCO (2005c) *Review of Comhairle na nÓg and Dáil na nÓg*. Available at www.omc.ie

NCO (2006) *Report of the Public Consultation for the development of a Recreation Policy for Young People (aged 12-18)*, National Children's Office. Dublin: The Stationery Office.

NCO, Children's Rights Alliance and National Youth Council of Ireland (2005) *Young Voices: Guidelines on how to involve children and young people in your work*, National Children's Office. Dublin: The Stationery Office.

NCTE (2002) *Be Wise on the Net Campaign. Information and Advice for Schools*. Dublin: National Centre for Technology in Education.

NDA (2005) *Promoting the participation of people with disabilities in physical activity and sport in Ireland*. Dublin: National Disability Authority.

NDA (2006) *Code of Practice on Accessibility of Public Services and Information provided by Public Bodies under the Disability Act 2005*. Dublin: National Disability Authority.

NESF (2003) *The Policy Implications of Social Capital. Forum Report No. 28, May 2003*. Dublin: National Economic and Social Forum.

Ní Laoire, C. (2001) 'A matter of life or death? Men, masculinities and staying 'behind' in rural Ireland', *Sociologia Ruralis*, Vol. 41, No. 2, pp. 220-36.

North Western Health Board (2004) *Consultations with teenage girls on being and getting active.* Ballyshannon: Health Promotion Department.

NYCI (2003a) *Art in their lives: A policy on young people and the arts.* Dublin: National Youth Council of Ireland.

NYCI (2003b) *National Youth Arts Programme Strategic Plan 2003-2006.* Dublin: National Youth Council of Ireland.

NYCI (2003c) *National Youth Arts Programme, IN2 Summer 2003.* Dublin: National Youth Council of Ireland.

NYCI (2004) *National Youth Arts Programme, IN2 Issue No. 6.* Dublin: National Youth Council of Ireland.

OMC (2006) *Report of the Public Consultation for the development of the National Recreation Policy for Young People*, Office of the Minister for Children. Dublin: The Stationery Office.

OMC (2007) *State of the Nation's Children, Ireland 2006*, Office of the Minister for Children. Dublin: The Stationery Office.

O'Neill, M. (2005) *Museums, galleries and young people: Are museums doing enough to attract young audiences?* Dublin: Proceedings of Symposium held on 4 November 2005.

Passmore, A. and French, D. (2001) 'Development and administration of a measure to assess adolescents' participation in leisure activities', *Adolescence*, Vol. 36, No. 141, pp. 67-69.

Pavis, S. and Cunningham-Burley, S. (1999) 'Male youth street culture: Understanding the context of health-related behaviours', *Health Education Research*, Vol. 14, No. 5, pp. 583-96.

Pedlar, A. (1995) 'The Role of Therapeutic Recreation', *Rehab & Community Care Management*, Vol. 4, No. 2, pp. 14-21.

Prince's Trust (2006) *Youth Cafés — Bringing communities closer.* London: The Prince's Trust.

Riddoch, C. (1998) 'Relationships between physical activity and physical health in young people', in *Young and Active? Young people and health-enhancing physical activity: Evidence and implications*, S. Biddle, J.F. Sallis and N. Cavill (eds.). London: Health Education Authority.

Royal Society for the Prevention of Accidents (2004) *Skateboarding: Safety Information Sheet Number 27.* Wantage: RoSPA Playground Management Ltd.

Ruddle, H. and Mulvihill, R. (1999) *Reaching Out: Charitable Giving and Volunteering in the Republic of Ireland.* Dublin: National College of Ireland.

Sallis, J.F., Zakarian, J., Hovell, M. and Hofstetter, C.R. (1996) 'Ethnic, socio-economic and sex differences in physical activity among adolescents', *Journal of Clinical Epidemiology*, No. 49, pp. 125-34.

Schwartz, K.D. and Fouts, G.T. (1998) 'Personality of adolescents and amount of time listening to music', Paper presented to the Western Psychological Association, Albuquerque, NM, April 1998.

Sinclair, R. (2004) 'Participation in practice — Making it meaningful, effective and sustainable', *Children and Society*, Vol. 18, No. 2, pp. 106-18.

Smith, P.G.R. and Therberge, J.B. (1987) 'Evaluating natural areas using multiple criteria: Theory and practice', *Environmental Management*, No. 11, pp. 447–60.

Smyth, E., Byrne, D. and Hannon, C. (2004) *The Transition Year Programme: An Assessment.* Dublin: Economic and Social Research Institute.

Steel, J.R. and Browne, J.D. (1995) 'Adolescent room culture: Studying the media in the context of everyday life', *Journal of Youth and Adolescence*, Vol. 24, No. 5, pp. 551-76.

Stiles, D.A., Gibbons, J.L. and Peters, E. (1993) 'Adolescents' views of work and leisure in the Netherlands and the United States', *Adolescence*, Vol. 28, No. 110, pp. 473-89.

Stone, E.J., McKenzie, T.L., Welk, G.J. and Booth, M.L. (1998) 'Effects of physical activity interventions in youth: Review and synthesis', *American Journal of Preventive Medicine*, Vol. 15, No. 4, pp. 298-315.

Thurlow, C. (2002) 'High-schoolers' peer orientation priorities: A snapshot', *Journal of Genetic Psychology*, No. 25, pp. 341-49.

Tiggerman, M. (2001) 'The impact of adolescent girls' life concerns and leisure activities on body dissatisfaction, disordered eating and self-esteem', *Journal of Genetic Psychology*, Vol. 162, No. 2, pp. 133-43.

UN (1989) *Convention on the Rights of the Child*. Geneva: United Nations Office of the High Commissioner for Human Rights. Available at www.ohchr.org

Valentine, G., Skelton, T. and Chambers, D. (1998) 'Cool Places: An introduction to youth and youth culture', in *Cool Places: Geographies of Youth Culture,* T. Skelton and G. Valentine (eds.). London: Routledge.

Van Vliet, W. (1983) 'Exploring the fourth environment: Home range of teenagers', *Environment and Behavior*, Vol. 15, No. 5, pp. 567-88.

Verma, S. and Larson, R.W. (2002) 'Television in Indian adolescents' lives: A member of the family', *Journal of Youth and Adolescence*, Vol. 31, No. 3, pp. 177-84.

Verma, S. and Larson, R.W. (eds.) (2003) *Examining Adolescent Leisure Time across Cultures. Developmental Opportunities and Risks: New Directions for Child and Adolescent Development, Special Issue, No. 99*. San Francisco: Jossey-Bass.

Weiss, J., Diamond, T., Demark, J. and Lovald, B. (2003) 'Involvement in Special Olympics and its relations to self-concept and actual competency in participants with developmental disabilities', *Journal of Applied Research in Intellectual Disabilities*, Vol. 24, No. 4, pp. 281-305.

Woods, C., Foley, E., O'Gorman, J., Kearney, J. and Moyna, N. (2005) *The Take Part Study: Physical Activity Research for Teenagers. Report for the Irish Heart Foundation, the Health Service Executive and Fingal Sports Partnership by School of Health and Human Performance, Dublin City University*. Dublin: Dublin City University.

WHO (2002) *The World Health Report 2002: Reducing risks, promoting health*. Geneva: World Health Organization.

WHO (2003) *The World Health Report 2003: Shaping the Future*. Geneva: World Health Organization.

Young Social Innovators (2006) *The Young Social Innovators '06 National Showcase Booklet*. Dublin: Young Social Innovators.

Youniss, J., McLellan, J.A. and Strouse, D. (1994) ' "We're popular but we're not snobs": Adolescents describe their crowds', in *Personal relationships during adolescence*, R. Montemayor, G. Adams and T. Gullotta (eds.). Thousand Oaks, CA: Sage.

Youth Work Ireland (2004) *A Guide to Quality Standards in Youth Services.* Dublin: Youth Work Ireland.

appendix one

Role of Government departments and agencies

Department of Arts, Sport and Tourism

The Department of Arts, Sport and Tourism is responsible for the administration of the Sports Capital Programme, which provides National Lottery Funding towards the development of local, regional and national facilities. The Department provides capital grants to club-owned facilities, community groups, national governing bodies of sport, third-level institutions and local authorities to improve or develop sports facilities. In the period 1998 to 2005, a total of €395 million has been allocated under the Sports Capital Programme to 4,923 projects nationwide across a range of sports and a variety of voluntary and community organisations, including sports clubs. The funding has assisted sports clubs and community organisations to provide a network of high-quality indoor and outdoor facilities for a wide range of sports and leisure facilities. The Department also operates the Local Authority Swimming Pool Programme, where €93 million has been allocated to public swimming pools under the current round of the programme between 2000 and April 2006. Investment has also been undertaken on major national venues, such as the National Aquatic Centre (€71m).

The Irish Sports Council

The Irish Sports Council's role is to 'plan, lead and co-ordinate the sustainable development of competitive and recreational sport in Ireland'. The Council works in partnership with other agencies, including the Department of Education and Science. It is also working on the development of local sports programmes though Local Sports Partnerships (which include local authorities, Vocational Education Committees, sports clubs, health boards and educational institutions). Since its establishment in 1999, €161 million has been provided to the Irish Sports Council to fund programmes to develop sport in Ireland. These include Local Sports Partnerships, many of which cater for young people, as well as grants to the governing bodies of sport to encourage underage participation.

The Arts Council

The Arts Council works with youth services to provide opportunities for self-expression among young people. The Council works closely with the Department of Education and Science, and the National Youth Council of Ireland. There is a National Youth Arts Programme, operated through the National Youth Council of Ireland, which deals primarily with arts programmes in the youth services sector. There are also Arts Officers based in the local authorities.

Department of Community, Rural and Gaeltacht Affairs

The Department of Community, Rural and Gaeltacht Affairs has responsibility for a number of schemes that facilitate the provision of youth services at local level. These schemes provide funding for youth services and facilities and are typically targeted at children at risk of social exclusion and/or drug misuse.

The Department funds the Young People's Facilities and Services Fund to assist in the development of youth facilities (including sport and recreational facilities) and services in areas where a significant drug problem exists, or has the potential to develop, and to attract 'at risk' young people into these facilities and activities and divert them away from the dangers of substance abuse. Funding is also provided for Sports Development Officers in each of the Task Force areas. The main focus of the work of the Sports Development Officers is in developing sport and recreational programmes to attract 'at risk' youth. The main focus of the Fund to date has been in Local Drugs Task Force areas, with a total of €106 million allocated to these so far.

Money is also provided under a range of other programmes which do not have a recreation focus, but which include a recreation dimension. These include the Community Development Programme, where €22.4 million was allocated in 2005; the Local Development Social Inclusion Programme, which spent €42.5 million; and the Dormant Accounts Fund, where up to €5.5 million has been allocated in 2006 to initiatives for disadvantaged young people with a recreation dimension.

Department of Justice, Equality and Law Reform

The Department of Justice, Equality and Law Reform funds projects under the Probation and Welfare system, as well as the Garda Juvenile Diversion Programme which aims to divert young people from taking part in criminal activities. In 2005, €5.47 million was spent on these projects (along with seven Local Drugs Task Force Projects). The Department also has responsibility in relation to policy on issues such as Garda vetting and disability.

Department of Education and Science

The Department of Education and Science is responsible for the school curriculum, including physical education (PE) in schools as well as PE/sports facilities. PE is not, however, compulsory at secondary level. The Transition Year Programme offers opportunities for the development of independent leisure skills among participating students through a variety of innovative programmes and projects. Schools also work in cooperation with the HSE in supporting the physical health component of the Social, Personal and Health Education (SPHE) Programme.

Opportunities are also provided through extra-curricular programmes for sport and recreation (e.g. chess and drama). The Department is collaborating with local authorities to explore the possibility of providing shared school and community facilities on new school campuses.

The Department is responsible for the sports facilities in schools. It is also responsible for a policy framework and financial support for youth work services. These deal with the personal and social development of young people outside of, but complementary to, formal education. The services, in the main, are delivered by national and regional voluntary youth services, such as Foróige, the National Youth Federation, Ógras Chorcaí and Catholic Youth Care, and in relation to one service in particular, the Special Projects for Disadvantaged Youth Scheme, by such organisations in close cooperation with the VECs. In 2005, €33.9 million was provided for this purpose through the operation of a range of funding schemes for youth work initiatives that included the Disadvantage Youth Scheme, the Youth Services Grant Scheme and the network of Youth Information Centres.

Funding for the youth work sector is not limited to the Department of Education and Science. The Department of Community, Rural and Gaeltacht Affairs supports youth-related activities through a variety of schemes, including the Community Development Programme, the Family and Community Services Programme and the Scheme of Grants for Voluntary Organisations. The youth work sector also obtains funding from the Department of Justice, Equality and Law Reform, as well as from the HSE and FÁS and through its own fund-raising.

Vocational Education Committees

The vocational education sector plays an important role in youth work and is ideally placed to respond effectively to local youth work needs. Currently, Vocational Education Committees (VECs) administer the Local Youth Club Grant Scheme on behalf of the Department of Education and Science. In addition, funding is provided to 8 VECs for the support of Youth Information Centres; to 17 VECs for the support, administration, development, monitoring and evaluation of Special Projects for Youth; and to 8 VECs for the administration of the Young Person's Facilities and Services Fund.

In some instances, VECs provide delivery of youth work programmes directly, e.g. City of Dublin Youth Service Board, which was established by City of Dublin VEC to support the development of youth work in Dublin City, and Waterford Youth Committee, which is a sub-committee of Waterford City VEC.

The Youth Work Act 2001 outlines the specific role of VECs with regard to the coordination, provision and development of youth work. VECs will be given an expanded role and will be required to prepare a 3-year youth work development plan for their administrative areas. This will enable VECs to assume specific new responsibilities with regard to the youth work programmes and/or services in their areas by coordinating their plans, proposals and activities.

Department of the Environment, Heritage and Local Government

The Department of the Environment, Heritage and Local Government has responsibilities through the local authorities for play and recreation programmes and facilities. It also provides certain grants to local authorities to assist with the provision of footpaths, cycleways and traffic-calming measures on public roads. In 2005, the Department provided almost €20 million for communal facilities in voluntary housing schemes, the development and improvement of public libraries and community centres, and the provision of playground and skateboard parks.

Local Authorities

The local authorities provide, operate and maintain parks and open spaces for amenity and recreation purposes. These include football pitches, tennis courts and playgrounds in both parks and housing complexes. They administer swimming pools provided under the Local Authority Swimming Pool Programme. Local authorities are the monitoring agency for the Young People's Facilities and Services Fund, which contributes to the construction, development and management of sports/youth/community centres. A number of local authorities have acquired land in scenic and rural areas which accommodate a range of active recreational facilities. Local authorities provide other opportunities for recreation and leisure through, for example, the Public Library Service.

There are Play Development Officers and Sports Development Officers in a number of local authorities. There are also Arts Officers based in 33 local authorities, administering a variety of programmes, some of which are targeted at young people.

Local authorities also support summer projects and summer activities for children and young people, many of which are organised by local volunteers.

Most City and County Development Boards, which have a role in implementing the National Children's Strategy, have incorporated play and recreation in their Strategies for Economic, Social and Cultural Development.

At local level, the local authorities have discretionary powers under the Local Government Act 2001 to incur expenditure to promote the interests of the local community in relation to general recreation and leisure activities, as well as sports, games and similar activities. In 2005, almost €817 million was provided to local authorities in general purpose grants from the Local Government Fund, from which they can fund community recreation projects. As indicated above, local authorities also receive money under the Sports Capital Programme, the Local Authority Swimming Pool Programme and the Department of Community, Rural and Gaeltacht Affairs. The Arts Council also part-funds Arts Officers in several local authorities.

The Planning and Development Act 2000 empowers local authorities to levy development contributions from builders as a condition of planning permission. These contributions can be used for capital costs associated with a wide range of public infrastructure and facilities, including the provision of open spaces, recreational and community facilities, and amenities and landscaping works. Planning authorities are obliged to draw up a development contribution scheme in respect of public infrastructure and facilities provided by, or on behalf of, the local authority that benefit development in the area.

Department of Health and Children

The Department of Health and Children has responsibility at policy level for promoting the health and well-being of the population, including young people, as outlined in the National Health Strategy and the National Health Promotion Strategy 2000-2005. The Health Service Executive has responsibility for the implementation and coordination of health promotion policy in a range of settings and across population groups. Physical Activity Coordinators promote physical activity among young people, including a number of specific programmes targeting teenage girls. Funding is also provided for a number of alcohol-free venues for young people, such as The Gaf in Galway and Elmo's Attic in Sligo.

Health Service Executive

The Health Service Executive (HSE) implements and coordinates health promotion policy in a range of settings and across population groups. Over the lifetime of the Cardiovascular Health Strategy, the Health Promotion Unit and the Health Service Executive have made significant investment in promoting physical activity for children and young people, including the appointment of 12 Physical Activity Coordinators, and structures have been put in place to provide advice and support in a number of settings, including schools, workplaces and communities, targeting in particular the young and older people.

Department of Transport

The Department of Transport is responsible for the Rural Transport Initiative which, among other things, is exploring the transport needs of young people in rural areas. The Department is involved with a number of initiatives to promote public transport that can help to create a healthier and safer environment for young people. Among these is a Traffic Management Guidelines Manual, which provides guidance for local authorities, developers, Government departments and An Garda Síochána on a variety of issues, including traffic planning, traffic calming and management, the incorporation of speed restraint measures in new residential designs and the provision of suitably designed facilities for public transport users and vulnerable road users.

appendix two

Membership of the Steering Group overseeing the development of the National Recreation Policy

Steering Group

Ms. Mary Golden, Chairperson	Office of the Minister for Children
Mr. Gerard Banville[1]	Office of the Minister for Children
Ms. Olive McGovern	Department of Health and Children
Mr. Denis Breen	Department of Arts, Sport and Tourism
Ms. Loretta Ní Mhaoldomhnaigh	Department of the Environment, Heritage and Local Government
Ms. Doreen Burke[2]	Department of Education and Science
Ms. Rachel Sheehan[3]	Department of Justice, Equality and Law Reform
Ms. Jeanette Young[4]	Department of Community, Rural and Gaeltacht Affairs
Ms. Eilis O'Connor[5]	Department of Communications, Marine and Natural Resources
Ms. Bernie Priestley[6]	Irish Sports Council
Mr. Karl Mitchell	Dublin City Council
Mr. Frank Dawson	Galway County Council
Ms. Janet Gaynor	Health Service Executive
Mr. Stephen O'Brien, Secretary	Office of the Minister for Children

[1] Mr. Gerard Banville replaced Ms. Alison Keogh, Office of the Minister for Children

[2] Ms. Doreen Burke replaced Mr. John Dolan, Department of Education and Science

[3] Ms. Sheelagh McAuliffe acted as an alternate for Ms. Rachel Sheehan, Department of Justice, Equality and Law Reform

[4] Ms. Jeanette Young substituted for Mr. Pádraig de Stanlaigh, Department of Community, Rural and Gaeltacht Affairs

[5] Mr. Michael O'Dwyer acted as an alternate for Ms. Eilis O'Connor, Department of Communications, Marine and Natural Resources

[6] Ms. Bernie Priestley replaced Ms. Ann Marie Hughes, Irish Sports Council